EXPERT PROFILES
VOLUME 11

Conversations with Influencers & Innovators

Linda Barnicott

Alexis Jane

Gail Dixon

LaWanna Bradford

Jason Gardner

Donna Singer

Claire E. Jones

Lindsay Andreotti

Denise Miller

Paula Jean Ferri

Joe Grushkin

Jerry Kezhaya

Mike Stewart

Royalties from the Retail Sales of "Expert Profiles" are donated to Global Autism Project

AUTISM KNOWS **NO BORDERS;**
FORTUNATELY NEITHER DO WE.®

Global Autism Project 501(c)3, is a nonprofit organization which provides training to local individuals in evidence-based practices for individuals with autism.

Global Autism Project believes that every child has the ability to learn and their potential should not be limited by geographical bounds.

The Global Autism Project seeks to eliminate the disparity in service provision seen around the world by providing high-quality training to individuals providing services in their local community. This training is made sustainable through regular training trips and contiguous remote training.

You can learn more about Global Autism Project by visiting GlobalAutismProject.org.

Table of Contents

Painter of Memories

Linda Barnicott began her career as a portrait artist in 1975. Today she is beloved and sought-after for her enchanting portraits of Pittsburgh. Using rich pastel colors, she captures the unique beauty of famous Pittsburgh scenes with a charm all her own. It began in 1989 with the now-famous tribute to downtown holiday shopping entitled "Meet Me Under Kaufmann's Clock." The work immediately won the hearts of Pittsburghers, who have been meeting friends under the clock downtown for years. From this work Linda created several series of Pittsburgh landmarks, capturing warm memories that are loved by generations. In 1995, she began painting a collection of Kennywood Park scenes that has become even more popular. Since then, she has brought to life the magic of every amusement park in the region, including Story Book Forest, Idlewild Park, Sandcastle Water Park and West View Park.

Linda is a powerhouse who is known as the "painter of memories." She is a self-taught painter. She was commissioned by the American Cancer Society of Pittsburgh for over 17 years to create a painting for their annual holiday cards. She also received a special proclamation from the City of Pittsburgh commemorating her tremendous contribution by capturing and preserving many sites in and around the Pittsburgh in soft pastel chalks.

Conversation with Linda Barnicott

Tell us a little bit about your background and how you got started and where you are today.

Linda Barnicott: I grew up on the other side of the state in a little suburb outside of Philadelphia, called Eddington. Drawing, for me, was my little "zone" growing up. I taught myself how to draw. I was fascinated with people's faces, so I would draw portraits and that took me all the way through my school years and into adulthood where I picked up soft pastels. I used to sit in front of a gallery and paint portraits of their customers. After I was finished the painting, the gallery would mat and frame them. One day, the owner asked me if I would do a painting of a streetcar. I said I had never drawn a streetcar or building in my life, but I did it!

While my husband was in seminary, I had a job downtown and my bus stop was under Kaufmann's Clock. So, I decided if I'm going to paint a streetcar, I needed to include Kaufmann's Clock since I knew it so well. At that point I had learned that for generations people met there. That was my first Pittsburgh painting. I went from portraits to painting Pittsburgh's city scenes in 1989.

"Meet Me Under Kaufmann's Clock" was really interesting because it was the first time I had ever drawn a building and of course it looked like it was going to fall over. I was fortunate enough to live next door to a graphic artist. He would spend hours teaching me how to make sure the building didn't look like it was going to fall down. There were a lot of tears, trust me, hours and hours that went into learning perspective—because it's totally different from portraits. Once I finished drawing it, I could paint it. Once I finished painting it and sales took off, I found myself with an unexpected career of painting Pittsburgh.

For people that are reading that are not from Pittsburgh, Kaufmann's Clock is a well-known landmark here and this is what Linda has become known for — her original painting, "Meet Me Under Kaufmann's Clock." So, do you still love painting? What do you like painting best right now?

Linda Barnicott: I love it all! Recently, I have returned to painting Pittsburgh. I just took a 10-painting hiatus and created a Santa Claus series. It was a great journey because it brought the portraits back into my life again. In each of the bigger paintings of Santa I always added a touch of Pittsburgh.

Is it more difficult to paint people and portraits than to draw buildings?

Linda Barnicott: Many artists tell me that they can't draw people. But, for me, it was the opposite. I was so in love with people's faces and their eyes. It was very natural for me to paint or draw people. That is why you see people in my paintings, it's rarely just buildings. People give the city its personality.

I've heard that you always draw a "certain someone" in your paintings – is that true?

Linda Barnicott: In "Meet Me Under Kaufmann's Clock," everybody in that painting was made up. Except, I needed somebody in the display window looking like they were hanging a wreath. I said to my husband one day in my studio, "Can you look like you're like standing, reaching up as if your hanging a wreath in the window? So, just like that, I drew him in the painting. He was my one person that was real.

When I designed my second painting of the University of Pittsburgh's Cathedral of Learning, there was a fellow that I included on the bench. My plan was to paint a rainy scene with a beautiful sunset in the background, like experiencing college, times which include difficulties and struggles but a new brighter day at the end.

But then I realized the person on the bench looked like he was getting rained on. So I removed him from the scene. My husband said to me, "Now you have a hole in your composition, you need somebody there." I said, "Okay, you go put on your raincoat and your hat and sit in a chair and I'll paint you so that it looks like you are sitting on the bench."

By the time I started painting the third painting, I was doing artist signings for the Cathedral of Learning and customers were asking, "Where are you putting your husband in your next painting?" I didn't even know they knew. I came home and told Tom, "They're expecting you to be in all my paintings!" Once again, he put on his coat and rain hat and he stood against the dining room wall. I drew him as if he was standing on the corner of the building. This started a tradition of painting him into all of my pieces, a lot like Alfred Hitchcock's cameos.

I love it. It's personal, but public for everyone to see. You've done so many winter scenes – why is that?

Linda Barnicott: The first six that I painted were fall/winter because they were released in the fall/early wintertime and that's a very romantic time of year. In 1998, I was painting summer scenes of Kennywood. I was at the Home and Garden show and somebody who was a representative of the American Cancer Society approached me and asked if I would draw their holiday card for the Pittsburgh chapter. Little did I know that moment it would provide 17 years of work for their holiday greeting card. They earned $750,000 just from the Christmas cards. Unfortunately, at the 17-year mark, they chose to close the program down as fewer people chose to send holiday cards.

One of my favorite things that you paint is Kennywood Amusement Park. You have done several drawings at Kennywood. Tell me a little bit about how you started doing those.

Linda Barnicott: In 1977, my eventual husband decided to take me to Kennywood for our first official Pittsburgh date. I remember walking by the carousel and seeing on older man standing on it as it whirled around. Tom said, "Oh, he has been here as long as I can remember and he's always taken the tickets for the Carousel." Years later, I would paint him in my first Kennywood painting, "Ride with Me on the Carousel', standing backwards while riding the carousel, kind of leaning out. His name was Tony Sacramento and he rode that carousel for 60 years. They called him Mr. Kennywood.

In 1995, I created the opportunity to paint Kennywood. It was a dream I had had since I first stepped into the park. I called Rick Sebak from WQED. He had just finished his film, "Kennywood Memories" and I asked him how to go about getting permission to paint the park. He told me, "You need to call Mary Lou Rosemeyer, and tell her I said, 'hi'."

I remember being so nervous. I took a deep breath and called her up and said, "I am a Pittsburgh artist. I'd really like to do some paintings of Kennywood because, personally, it's part of my memories. Her response was, "That would be wonderful!" That was the start of my 10-year trek painting Kennywood. I pretty much documented everything in the park except the bumper cars.

Are they still there?

Linda Barnicott: When I started sketching the Carousel, my youngest daughter, who was four at the time, walked into my studio at home. She peeked up at my work and said, "Where are you going to put Brittany and me?"

I could do that, I thought. I bet she overheard her daddy and me tell folks that I painted him in all of my paintings. I was excited! I called Mary Lou Rosemeyer at the park, and invited a whole bunch of family and friends. We all met at the Carousel on opening day in May of 1995. After posing people on the ride I took a hundred photographs and I worked from those photographs. It would be the first time everybody in my painting would be a real person that I knew, and from that point on I would only use real models.

If I contacted you to do a painting where I wanted to be drawn into the painting, would you have a problem doing that?

Linda Barnicott: I actually have done that over the years. I've had people want to be a model in a painting and it's no problem.

It would make a good gift too; with all the holidays, like Mother's Day, Father's Day, birthdays and all the things you can think of where a unique gift would be perfect.

Linda Barnicott: I have a friend who's in real estate and she and her family are in one of my paintings. It is another painting of Kaufmann's Clock called, "Waiting for you Under Kaufmann's Clock." Every time she sells a house, she has me frame up one of those mini prints in an 8" x 10" frame. I write a special message on the back and sign the front glass in gold in the right bottom corner. She gives it to her customers as a housewarming gift.

Another example is, Ameriprise has used my paintings as their sales awards each year and the award winner could earn a different painting every year. The framer would create a cutout in the mat and we would add their name and what their sales award was for. It was cool being a part of their day and personally signing the prints for them at the event.

Have you ever painted anybody famous?

Linda Barnicott: I've had really cool opportunities over the years. One of them was Bill Mazeroski who was part of the greatest baseball event of the century. In 1960, his world-famous home run against the New York Yankees earned the Pittsburgh Pirates the World Series. If you talk to Mazeroski, his comment is, "I was a great second baseman, but I was never a hitter." He says that was a fluke.

"I should've never gotten the attention that I got for that." He's a very modest, very kind, loving man and for me, it was a great experience.

Anyone else?

Linda Barnicott: Pittsburgh Steeler Franco Harris! In 2012, I created, "Franco Harris and the Story of the Immaculate Reception," which captured what has been called the greatest play in NFL history. What was really neat about Franco was that we were text buddies. My kids were going nuts because Franco was texting me and I was texting him back. He worked with me throughout the entire project, which was really cool. As I would paint part of the piece, I would send it to him and get his response. If I needed to make a few corrections, I could do that. It was really, really wonderful. We unveiled it at his private party at the History Center where Tom and I got to meet a whole bunch of the 1972 Steelers. I remember when we left and were walking to the parking lot, that I elbowed Tom and said, "Aren't you glad you married me?" I mean, he just got a chance to meet all of his heroes from childhood.

So, tell us about your biggest project?

Linda Barnicott: Hands down, it was Forbes Hospital in Monroeville, PA. They now have a 4-foot by 40-foot history wall. It's made up of five panels. Each one was 4x8. They had the unveiling on November 6th 2019, it was amazing. The project lasted a long time. I think I signed the contract in 2014. It was a lot of work. I managed to put my husband on the fifth panel, riding in one of the UPMC healthy ride bikes. It was a lot of fun. Of course, I had to paint him in somewhere.

When anyone looks at your paintings, the detail on them is incredible. I can't imagine five panels that huge and your detail, that it would take you any less time than 4 years. That's absolutely incredible.

Linda Barnicott: The wall was made up of five different themes. It started with the historical beginning which included fundraising for the hospital. The second panel was called the "Faces of Care" featuring all the people who volunteered, the nurses, the doctors, hospice, etc. The middle panel featured the community and the interfaith ministries in Monroeville. The fourth panel I created Forbes Hospital as it is today. The last panel captured Forbes within the Allegheny Health Network's hospital system. I have to say, they couldn't have been nicer throughout the whole project.

Which is your favorite painting?

Linda Barnicott: I have different favorite paintings in different series – the Santa series, the Pittsburgh series, Kennywood series. But I think my ultimate favorite is called "Coasting Through Kennywood." Back in 1977 on that first Pittsburgh date, Tom and I had only known each other three months, we talked over the phone and he had visited me twice. That weekend my husband decided to propose to me. He'd been nervously hinting at it all day. We were on the bridge overlooking a beautiful lagoon watching old aluminum boats floating by when I told him about dreams I had had earlier in the week that we got engaged and married. He got this stunned look on his face and just walked away, leaving me on the bridge alone. I thought "Oh, what did I say? Oh my gosh."

Well fortunately for me, the next night, five minutes before the last call for my flight to go back home, he proposed to me and it started our big long-distance engagement. Also, in this painting are tons of my favorite people. On the right side is my husband and my daughters, and you'll notice the boats are numbered. I don't know if Kennywood ever had a number 22 but it was my husband's sales number when he sold shoes at South Hills Village Mall in Upper St. Clair. He had a habit or writing his number 22 on some dollar bills. The very first time we met, he came out to New Jersey with me and we were on this college trip where I was up in the woods tearing down a bunch of small buildings, trying to make an artist colony. We took a break and in the middle of the woods we came across this little ice cream stand called Dilly's and we ordered food. When we received the change there was a dollar bill that had Tom's handwriting and a number 22 on it.

Those are just a few reasons I love this painting.

Can you tell us about painting plein air landscapes?

Linda Barnicott: I do a lot of city scenes where it's cement, cement, cement, but I always got in trouble when it came to something that had a lot of green in it – green trees, green grass, green bushes. I was getting a little bit burnt out from painting all the Pittsburgh scenes and I decided I needed to change. I took some workshops with Richard McKinley, who is a brilliant plein air landscape artist from Oregon. I loved his paintings and the colors sang to my soul. I tried to get into a workshop, and when I called they said, "Great, you're number 41 on the waiting list!"

So, I tried another, and I was 20 on the list. I tried another and I was 11 and I thought, "Maybe I'll get into that one!" The first time I met Richard was in New York City. He gave us a list of materials, pastels, and paper I'd never used before. I was always a studio painter and here I was showing with materials I didn't even recognize. Funny thing, after New York I got a call from another workshop.

This time I went to the state of Washington and spent a nine-day bootcamp with him. Soon after I came home, I received another call and took a 3rd workshop three hours from my home in Penn State. Three workshops in one year!

I painted 18 original plein air landscape pieces that year, creating a roaming original art show in four different galleries over four months. My city scenes became fresh after that and my portraits too! When learning new techniques, you tend to waffle a little bit back and forth trying to find your own way, but when you figure it out you come back stronger than you were before.

Tell us a little bit about your Pittsburgh Tunnel painting and how that one got inspired and started.

Linda Barnicott: This is a new painting. I just finished it in the spring. It's called "Pittsburgh Tunnel Vision." Let me tell you about my first experience in Pittsburgh. Tom picked me up at the airport and he was talking to me as we're driving through Robinson, which wasn't really a town then. It was mostly woods and green trees at the time. Growing up in Pennsylvania, I've driven through tunnels before – just more green trees and hills on the other side. As we were driving, we came across a tunnel and Tom just kept chatting away, not telling me that anything was going to happen. He let me really experience it. We drove out of the tunnel and it was like the whole world felt like it just fell away.

There was all this steel, all this shiny metal everywhere! I was enthralled with all the buildings. From the time I started painting Pittsburgh, I thought of that first vision. For years I've wanted to paint that view. Recently, I met up with a photographer friend at a gallery. He was showing me pictures on his phone and he had some photographs from up above the tunnels looking into town. I said, "Oh my gosh, this is the picture I've been wanting to paint all my life!" He said, "You know what, Linda, you can use my work." So, I took several different photographs that he had taken and used them as resources to create this painting.

Everybody who travels to Pittsburgh or visits Pittsburgh goes through the Fort Pitt Tunnel and comes out to see this sight. It is the most spectacular view, especially if it's twilight and the city lights are just coming on. The barges are cruising down the river, over to the left is Heinz Field, PNC Park and the Point fountain. It really is an amazing experience to take in.

I've had so much positive feedback from my customers. I've heard many great stories of people who are touched by this view because it helps them remember that special moment when they met Pittsburgh.

I love that you write a blog every week to share your journey through your paintings, telling readers about the progress and what you're going through.

Linda Barnicott: I've had a lot of requests for the stories behind the paintings and I started to write them down. My goal is eventually someday to have that coffee table book with the stories that go along with the paintings. I am actually working on a new book. I am creating a book based on the Jolly Old Elf series. It will feature each painting and include a story about the inspiration behind the painting, and also the backstory on why I created it, how I created it, and a couple other fun facts. I'm hoping to have it out for this holiday season.

Oh wow. Well that's ambitious when you do all of these works of art, I can't even imagine how many hours that you put into these. So, between that and the book, I'd say you're a little busy over there. Do you do commission work?

Linda Barnicott: I do take commissions for original art. I have a project coming up to paint, "The Ship of the Alleghenies," which was actually a hotel/restaurant built to resemble a ship, up in the mountains along Route 30. I'm also planning to paint a couple more pieces this year for my Pittsburgh series including the Original Hotdog Shop, a landmark in Oakland. Sadly, they recently closed which puts it into the realm of nostalgia now. I am in the process of sketching it.

Also, Tom and I have talked a lot about painting a scene from the North Shore which would include the very moving Police Memorial to fallen officers. Sculptures of an officer and police dog gaze across the river at downtown Pittsburgh. The working title I have for it right now is "Watching over Pittsburgh." I'm probably going to paint it as a night scene because of the beautiful glow of the lights in the water.

Where is your studio located?

Linda Barnicott: I live in Brentwood, Pennsylvania. We have an old, unique 1935 house. The whole basement floor is my studio. The entire house has my artwork and my art supplies in it. The living room and dining room house all my original paintings so, when customers come, they walk right into my gallery.

If somebody wants to reach out to you, either to buy prints or get an original or commission, how would you like them to reach you?

Linda Barnicott: Email me at linda@lindabarnicott.com or sign up for my newsletter on my website. Just put it in a first name and an email and then they'll get to see the progression of the paintings and stay up to date with everything going on.

On my website at LindaBarnicott.com I not only have paintings, but I have lots of gift ideas including coasters, mint trays, ornaments, bookmarks and more.

About Linda Barnicott

Linda Barnicott began her career as a portrait artist in 1975. Today she is beloved and sought-after for her enchanting portraits of Pittsburgh. Using rich pastel colors, she captures the unique beauty of famous Pittsburgh scenes with a charm all her own. It began in 1989 with the now-famous tribute to downtown holiday shopping entitled "Meet Me Under Kaufmann's Clock." The work immediately won the hearts of Pittsburghers, who have been meeting friends under the clock downtown for years. From this work Linda created several series of Pittsburgh landmarks, capturing warm memories that are loved by generations. In 1995, she began painting a collection of Kennywood Park scenes that has become even more popular. Since then, she has brought to life the magic of every amusement park in the region, including Story Book Forest, Idlewild Park, Sandcastle Water Park and West View Park, which closed in 1977.

With roots as a portrait artist, Barnicott includes family members and friends in every painting. "If you look carefully, you can watch my daughters grow up over the years, starting with the Kennywood Series," says Barnicott. "And my husband appears in just about all of them."

Barnicott was chosen to be the official artist of the 1996 Three Rivers Regatta. Since 1998, she has been commissioned by the American Cancer Society of Greater Pittsburgh to create the painting used on their annual holiday card. In 2000, Barnicott received a special Proclamation from the City of Pittsburgh, commemorating her "tremendous contribution in capturing and preserving many sites in and around the Pittsburgh Area." This is an honor she holds dear, as a largely self-taught artist.

In 2006, Linda's company, Linda Barnicott Publishing, LLC, was chosen as a winner of the prestigious 2006 Forbes® Enterprise Award. In March of 2008, she was honored to be a featured cover story of the national magazine, "Professional Artist." In 2010, Barnicott began an amazing partnership with Wendell August Forge. Based in Grove City, Pennsylvania, these artisans are known for their exquisite hand-made metal work and are currently creating a beautiful collection of ornaments from her beloved paintings. She also was invited to become a member of the esteemed Salmagundi Club in New York City, one of the oldest art organizations in the country.

Each year, Barnicott's endearing scenes become more popular. Her paintings and collectibles are sold worldwide, on the Internet and appear in regional galleries and gift shops. Whether it's paintings of Pittsburgh, sports arenas and players, landscapes, portraits or Santa Claus, she loves talking with her clients and hearing the memories that her paintings evoke. She is currently accepting commissioned original works and participates in numerous art shows throughout the year. There is a calendar of events on her website. Barnicott's studio is in Brentwood, Pennsylvania where she lives with her husband. You can visit an online gallery of all of her paintings at LindaBarnicott.com.

WEBSITE
LindaBarnicott.com

ADDRESS
Studio is By Appointment Only,
3211 Brownsville Road, Pittsburgh, PA 15227

PHONE
1 (888) 748-8278

EMAIL
linda@lindabarnicott.com

FACEBOOK
Facebook.com/LindaBarnicott

Shift Your Mindset to Attract All That You Desire

Alexis Jane... bestselling author and mindset coach! She's uplifting, inspiring and confident, everything you could want from a coach that helps entrepreneurs to perform at their peak, and with many previously satisfied clients, she's tried and tested.

Here for you is an eye-opening interview with Alexis. Is your business in a sticky situation, or perhaps your personal life? This interview will provide a solution to many problems you may be facing within your life. If clarity is what you're seeking, but you feel like past conditioning is an obstacle, make yourself comfortable and take a read. Hopefully, you take something from this and start applying it to your own personal and professional life.

Conversation with Alexis Jane

How did you find your calling in life? How did you know this is what you were born to do?

Alexis Jane: I was never really an academic at school, but I loved being social. I originally worked as a personal trainer and also within the hospitality and catering industry, so I was always around people. Then, I got married but, unfortunately, had a breakdown in my marriage and through that process, I found life coaching.

Through life coaching I found kinesiology, NLP hypnosis, time-line therapy and I didn't know that these existed. I just thought there were psychology counselors. I'd seen quite a few of them and I wasn't getting the results that I desired, so I went and studied life coaching. I was working mainly with people, helping them within the life coaching space, and from this, I found a passion for business.

It was interesting watching women growing businesses and helping them through their mindset hacks and figuring out what was keeping them stuck around their money mindset, their belief system, whether they thought they were self-worthy or how much self-love and self-esteem they had.

I go quite deep into patterning. So, what's the pattern that's kept you stuck from moving forward? When you're in that pattern, you don't really understand that it's actually a pattern or a cycle that's going on because you're so caught up in that moment.

How do you go from recognising the patterns to actually being able to clear them and stop them from affecting your actions?

Alexis Jane: First, you need to understand and know what your pattern is. If you're not sure what your pattern is or cycle is, one awesome activity or tool to use is doing a brain dump and journaling it out. Getting all of the surface noise out and when you're continually doing that on a daily basis, you start seeing what your pattern is and you start seeing your recurring thoughts that keep coming up.

Then, once you know what the thought process is, you can start to think how you would rather be living life opposed to having that thought process. For instance, if your main thought process is around lack of money or lack of clients coming into your business, what needs to happen for that to be a different mindset? So, if we go with the thought process of lack of money, a lack of money and scarcity will continue showing up. You want to start moving inch by inch.

Start being grateful for the things you've already got in your life. There's already money everywhere. If you're sitting in your house and looking around and you see your TV, that was created and purchased by money, so be thankful that you have a TV. Or be thankful that you actually have a house to live in. Once you start becoming thankful for the things you already have, more starts to show up in your life. If it's a deep-rooted belief around the lack of money, it does and will take time to switch and change that mindset.

What if someone doesn't know what they actually want? Would that process be the same?

Alexis Jane: One thing I find with a lot of my clients when I first start working with them is that when I ask them what they want, 95% say, "I don't know what I want."

So, in response to this I ask, "If you were to know what you want, what would that be?" They then start rambling on about the things they actually want but because we're conditioned to say 'I don't know;' it's the confidence behind what it is you want. So, if you say you want a $1,000,000 business, that's originally what you wanted to say. But the issue is you put up a block in front of that, and that block is – if I say I want a $1,000,000 business, what's the judgement that's going to be associated with that, what will people think of me?

It's all about having the confidence behind what it is that you want to then be able to go and do the aligned action to get there. So,

I'll now take you through the steps that I take my clients through to really uncover what it really is that they truly desire.

Start by asking yourself the following questions:

1. Where do you want to live?
2. What kind of home do you want to be living in?
3. What area?
4. Who do you want to associate yourself with, as in who do you want to hang out with?
5. Who do you want to be listening to on the radio or on podcasts?
6. Who is it that you really need to become to be able to live the life that you want to have?

Really own it. Be comfortable and confident to who that person is that you want to step into.

So, before we get what we want, we need to become that person first?

Alexis Jane: To become that person, you need to align yourself with that next-level version of yourself. It all equates to belief. I've found my clients struggle with the thought of who they really need to become.

Visualise yourself as your next level self and ask yourself questions similar to the following:

1. How do you need to stand now? Shoulders back, back straight and having that presence when you walk into a room.
2. Appearance is important, so what clothes are you wearing now? How are you styling your hair? Make up? How are you presenting yourself when you walk out of the house? How are you presenting yourself professionally?
3. How do you spend your time?
4. How do you eat? Do you work out?

5. How do you feel about yourself?

Everyone has different dreams and desires, but when you're stepping into who you need to become, what does that actually look like? It doesn't necessarily mean going out and buying a whole new wardrobe, it's utilizing what you've got and being comfortable and confident enough to do something that's a little bit different than what you've been doing in the past.

So, from this, how does someone know what action they need to take? Let's say they've already figured out who they need to become, where do they go now?

Alexis Jane: It's looking at the world in a different way and also going internal to your inner world. When you go into your inner world, there's lots of beliefs that start to pop up and lots of blocks start to present themselves.

So, once you actually start knowing who you are, the universe, God, spirit, a higher self, whatever it is that you choose to call it, will start presenting challenges or things that you need to work through that are going to help you move to the next level. So, the more that you're doing the inner work, the more you're creating space for yourself for goodness to come in, but it's how you choose to move through.

Journaling is an amazing tool to use. Using a brain dump to get all the noise out but then asking yourself a conscious question. That question is, "How do I want to show up for myself today?" And then, "How do I want to show up as being that new version of myself, what has to happen?"

When you ask yourself those questions after you've done a brain dump, things will start to flow through that you didn't even know were deep inside. Once you actually know who you want to become, you want to write a statement of what your dream life actually looks like and what it also feels like. You want to start believing that it can actually happen. When you look around, there's already lots of people out there that are doing things you want to be doing. So, if they can do it, you can do it as well!

So, you figure out exactly what it is that you want to do with the brain dump and the journaling, figure out who you want to become and what beliefs go along with that and start living alongside those beliefs, and have that mental image of this dream life you want, is that correct?

Alexis Jane: Yes! And really having trust and faith that it can happen when you start having a burning desire for the things that you truly deeply want. I'll explain the burning desire as it was a concept I originally struggled to get my head around, and I feel that may be the case with other people. If you haven't done anything like this before, when you initially start to visualize and feel it, it can be a little bit tricky to begin with because you've never felt that sensation before. You don't actually know what it feels like as you've never been there. So, it's taking the small steps into the feeling of it.

For example, what would having an additional $500 or $1,000 dollars a month feel like for you? I know for myself when I first started doing this, visualizing $1,000,000 was just way too big for me, but $100,000 was something that I could get a grasp on to then move through and start to visualize it.

I know people in my world that have that amount of money, they earn that amount, and are doing those things. So, modeling and watching what they're doing, so as you start to grow and you start to know what that feeling is, you can increase your money mindset and go to a higher level, but you've got to start somewhere.

If your gaps are too big, there's too much to bridge. You want to do small increments so as you start to build up, that'll be when you start seeing the shifting change, because it's not overwhelming. Start with a small gap, and gradually increase.

That makes sense! So, personally, I've seen a pattern this week and I'll share, because I'm sure someone reading this will resonate. I set myself big goals, ones that seem scary and I start sabotaging. Do you think that could be why I, or any reader who finds themselves in a similar pattern, is sabotaging? Setting a goal, with a humongous gap so that the belief hasn't had a chance to catch up with the outcome?

Alexis Jane: Yes. I can relate to that myself because I've done it before and that's why I worked out that I needed to reduce the size of the goal. Having a huge scary goal is awesome, but at the same time, you want to chunk it back. So, what has to happen before that huge goal is achieved, chunking it and working out what the aligned daily actions are, that have to be taken to get to that point.

In marketing, we talk about the need to have 7 to 12 touch points before someone likes and trusts you and will invest. However, I personally believe that within the digital world, it takes a little bit more, but for the sake of this explanation, we'll stick with the 7 to 12.

It's the same as what it is you desire. McDonald's is always in front of you somewhere. They've either got a poster, or an advertisement on the radio, they're everywhere. The same with Coca-Cola. But when you're doing your own goals, you should be marketing them to yourself every day. All day, every day!

Feeling it, visualizing it, talking about it. You want to have those 7 to 12 touch points within yourself around the goals that you want to achieve. When you know what your big scary goal is, write that down and make sure you have it with you all of the time.

Maybe even set an alarm for every hour that you're awake reminding you to look at this goal. This can help you feel and visualize it. Just look at it for 1 to 2 minutes every hour. Every time it's done, you will be reconnecting yourself to that goal. Eventually, it won't seem so big and scary. By putting it all into practice, the results will start to show a lot faster.

The universe will start pulling that plan together for you.

About Alexis Jane

Alexis Jane. You've just read her interview "Shift Your Mindset to Attract All That You Desire" and you want to know a little bit more about her.

A single mother, a professional businesswoman who loves challenging the status quo and shifting her clients mindsets into peak performance.

Her business revolves around helping her clients to achieve results, from being completely exhausted to confident, powerful leaders so they can operate at peak performance.

Through a variety of techniques and her own personal beliefs she digs deep, she finds the gaps and fills them with essential knowledge!

If you feel her services would complement your lifestyle, then get in contact her through one of the links listed below.

Let Alexis be the catalyst to the much-needed life change.

WEBSITE
Alexis-Jane.com

EMAIL
Alexis-Jane.com/Contact

FACEBOOK
Facebook.com/TheAlexisJane

INSTAGRAM
Instagram.com/TheAlexisJane

Finding Your Heart's Voice

Gail Dixon specializes in guiding people to name, frame and claim the verbal expression of their brand identity and core messaging. Her extensive experience, more than 30 years, combined with her unique gift of "listening between the lines" positions Gail as the top expert and trusted authority for personal and brand messaging. She is committed to serving speakers, authors, thought leaders, corporations, nonprofits and associations, and of course, mission driven entrepreneurs. If you're eager to have a greater impact in the world with your products and services, Gail will show you how to master your message and make your mark.

Conversation with Gail Dixon

How do you discover your heart's voice? What do you mean by that?

Gail Dixon: The heart's voice is the voice that each of us speaks and uses when we are at our best, purest, most authentic selves. It is the voice that we use to speak into the great unity of the world. I believe that before we're born, God whispers a message into each of our hearts, a truth. That is our unique piece, the piece that brings purpose and meaning to our lives, the thing we're meant to contribute to the world. The heart's voice is the voice that captures that and speaks that into the world.

Why is using your heart's voice so important in your messaging?

Gail Dixon: For three reasons. First, the heart's voice is the voice of truth and authenticity. I think that as we live in the world, sometimes we play roles. Sometimes we hide behind masks. Sometimes we don't fully claim who we are at the core. That truth and authenticity is important. Secondly, the heart's voice is the voice that connects us to others. It's not only important for us to speak from our heart's voice, but to listen with the heart's ear. That's the ear that listens with compassion, understanding, support, connection and community. And the third reason, in terms of why it's important, is that it is the voice that allows us to function at that highest level of growth and contribution in the world. It's the language of growth. It's the language of values. It's the language of affirmation. When we are living on purpose and in our purpose, and speaking with the voice that names that purpose, that's when we are giving the biggest meaning to our lives and when we're making the biggest contribution to the world.

So, what happens when people don't speak from their heart?

Gail Dixon: Many things happen. One is that of course, they miss connections with other people. They miss the mark. Their hopes, aspirations and dreams aren't fulfilled. Their relationships don't function well. Their goals are not met, because they're missing the mark and things don't line up in a global sense when we don't speak with the heart's voice. We have division and discrimination. We have destruction of the planet. We have all of those things that come from less than authentic, less than true, pure, heart voices and we also in some ways, deeply wound ourselves when we speak to ourselves or about ourselves with voices that are not heart- centered.

What is it about humans that keeps us from using our heart-centered communication all the time?

Gail Dixon: I think it is a natural thing to speak from the heart until we begin to get socialized. For example, think about the look that an infant sends its parents, the look in their eyes. They may not be using words, but they're speaking volumes, in terms of that adoration and that connection. Infants don't have anything that starts filtering and backing away from the truth. It's "I'm happy. I'm hungry. I'm cold. I'm wet. I'm sleepy." Those are the messages that they send, and they send them clear and direct, right out there. They don't start filtering and second guessing until they begin to get socialized.

First of all, we start to hear and understand other people's voices and when those people are not speaking to us from the heart, we begin to take on negative or false messages about ourselves... deep questions about our worth and worthiness. Fears in the world, anger, resentment, lack, confusion. All those messages start coming in. When we start hearing the voices of other people, it can add the voices of all those emotions that aren't right on that North Star pivot point of truth and authenticity. It makes it hard for us to hear the deep truth in us.

Very often, we play old tapes in our heads and we can hear things that are echoes of past hurts. I can remember – and it stayed with me a really, really, long time – that I had a Girl Scout leader in about the third or fourth grade. We were doing crafts in Girl Scouts and she said to me, "You have messy hands." She was she was talking about the fact that I was being sloppy. I wasn't gluing things on right or something. That tape plays in the back in my head. Anytime that I try to do something with my hands and I don't do it well, I think about that. Many of the tapes that run through our heads and our hearts are positive ones, but sometimes we hang on to some negative ones that can get in the way. Right now, in this particular time and place in the world, the voices that we have out there are the voices of fear, panic, dread, lack, anger, confusion and contradiction. It's hard to figure out what to hear and what to listen to. It's hard to sort out what the intent for some of that language is. It can make it hard for us to hear our own heart's voice and to hear the true voices of others or to discern whether they're speaking to us from the heart. Life can get in the way and while speaking with the heart's voice is something that we start off life with, we may lose ourselves along the way. But it's something that we can regain with attention and intention. And it's something that's well worth the effort.

How do we know when we're coming from our true message? What do we hear or feel that lets us know when we're in it?

Gail Dixon: I think about three things. For those of us who are visual, it is when we see in our mind's eye the smile, the confidence and that look of love. We see ourselves in our mind's eye as glowing, positive, loving and alive. We get an image of ourselves as we're speaking. For those of us who are more auditory. I think we hear when we're speaking with the heart's voice, when we hear the conviction, the intensity. When people are really solid and convinced about something sometimes their voices raise and get rapid and intense, and other people slip into speech that is lower, quieter and more deliberate. I speak lower, and slower when I'm speaking from my heart's voice, because I am feeling my heart and it fills my chest and I can feel that.

There are times when you can hear the conviction in someone's voice. For folks that are more tactile or kinesthetic, it's feeling the vibration. When you feel that high vibration that says, "Ooh, this is good," when you're not feeling conflicting vibrations, or dissonance, but feeling a positive high vibration. Or, when you feel solid and grounded in your body, that's when you're hearing or speaking from your heart. One of the phrases that sometimes gets used to describe how we know we're hearing something that comes from the heart is that of the "Zen arrow." It's something that comes purely from the source and goes right to our hearts. I think we recognize that when we don't get caught up in all those other conflicting voices. It's an act of intentional speaking and listening.

Once somebody really knows who they are and the master message that they're trying to convey—their heart message, how do we share it so that other people receive it properly?

Gail Dixon: We all use different modes of expression in our lives to connect and to say who we are. Some people for example, speak and share their heart's voice through their creative work, through music, art or dance. Some do it through their relationships or charitable work where their heart's voice speaks in terms of the good that they do for others, or in the nurturing of a child. Certainly, we know that, in terms of expressing our master message – that one core truth that's meant to bring meaning and purpose to our lives – people need to use their heart's voice. Still others do it through the way that they build and make connections and create community and contribute to the world.

I firmly believe that we all are little pieces of the Divine, and, as we as we evolve, we grow back to that. We're scattered as stars but at some point in Universal Time, we will be back to be united as one. Speaking and listening through and from the heart's voice is how we make our contribution, how we put our piece into the puzzle of the great unity.

If you had one thought or message that you would want people to carry with them as a result of working with you or hearing you speak, what would that be?

Gail Dixon: I would want to tell people that you are made to be a messenger of some specific, clear truth, that expresses your purpose and your meaning in the world, and that when you find and hear that truth and can express it into the world, that's when your life will be aligned on purpose and fulfilled.

If somebody wants to work with you, how do they connect with you?

Gail Dixon: I work in two streams. One is for the people who are looking to craft a message for the purpose of fulfilling a mission or in business or for a brand to express a clearer public identity. Then, for others for whom it's a more personal development kind of stream, those seeking to uncover and develop a message around: "What's my purpose?" I do some initial discovery, some of what I call "essential essence work" with folks trying to discern: "What's the core message?"

I work toward teaching people to hear it in themselves and for themselves, sorting through all the things that may keep them from hearing that. For anybody who is looking to express that, whether they are folks with big missions or purposes in business or, as part of a community of organizers and developers, we focus first on hearing the message for yourself. Then we work more with how to share that message so that others will receive and understand it. It's what we sometimes call "the dictionary" or "the lexicon" for your heart's voice.

We uncover: "What's the language that expresses your mission? What are the words that really resonate?" And then we connect and talk about, "What are the things that get in the way of that?" Everybody starts with learning to listen to themselves, because you have to sort out the heart's voice in yourself first. What we need to do is hear it, own it, and then take it out into the world.

I wanted to ask you a little bit about some of the things that that you were involved in. Weren't you involved in a global experience, making a movie?

Gail Dixon: I was involved with *Awakening Giants*, which was a group of folks with big missions— change makers, transformation agents. We have had several locations where up to 20 folks come together for an experience of mutual self-development and exploration of their missions and intentions in the world for mutual support and really challenging themselves and each other and doing local service. In San Diego, we did some work and fundraising for Wolf Connection, the wolf sanctuary where young men at risk come and learn the way of the wolf as a way of developing their own character. Some of the other projects have brought water to villagers in African countries. They're working at bringing a documentary television series together and also doing other changemaking kind of work.

One of the shifts that I've made just recently is recognizing that I had spent a lot of my time helping others to discover and express their messages and part of what I know now is that I'm meant to be the messenger about the importance of the heart's voice. I have to not just put other people on their stages with the right words, but I have to take the stage myself bringing the message about the importance of heart-centered messaging. I believe that at this point in our global life, we have gone astray with lots of those other voices and it's the heart's voice as a universal language that will bring healing to the world. My job is to tell the world how important that is.

To learn more, check out MasterfulMessaging.com. It is the heart's voice that will bring both fulfillment to your life individually and healing to the world. That's why it's important to listen and speak from that perspective.

About Gail Dixon

Gail Dixon is a five-time best-selling author and inspirational speaker. As a word wizard and brand positioning expert she has worked with hundreds of thought leaders, business experts, and up-and-coming change agents to name, frame and claim their personal and brand identities. Her gift of listening at the heart level positions Gail as a top expert and trusted authority for creating messaging that commands attention, creates connection and ignites impact. In 2017, Gail was selected as one of 100 "Awakening Giants," a group of leaders working to inspire conscious leadership to positively impact 88 million lives worldwide.

WEBSITE
MasterfulMessaging.com

EMAIL
gail@masterfulmessaging.com

FACEBOOK
Facebook.com/Gail.Dixon.94

LINKEDIN
LinkedIn.com/in/GailDixonMessaging

YOUTUBE
YouTube.com/results?search_query=gail+dixon+masterful+messaging

INSTAGRAM
Instagram.com/GailDDixon

Strategic Planning for Your Success

LaWanna Bradford is a serial entrepreneur and global leader in the strategic planning and performance management arena. She is a thought leader and business management consultant who applies strategic thinking and business management concepts to maximize efficiency and effectiveness and identify both business and life opportunities for improvement and growth. She is the COO of The Bradford Group, a commercial and investment mortgage brokerage, and the Principal of Bradford Group Consulting, a business management consulting firm. As a change agent, she leverages her 30-plus years of experience working with federal and private industries and small businesses to guide individuals toward achieving growth, understanding their market position, and increasing awareness of the customers they serve.

Though based in Atlanta, GA, The Bradford Group (TBG) serves homeowners, business owners and investors nationally and internationally. The company's mission is to help customers achieve a piece of the American dream through delivering excellent mortgage purchasing and refinancing services. In today's market, many homeowners, small business owners, investors, and foreign national borrowers are seeking loan programs that allow flexibility and customization. The Bradford Group understands that going directly to a bank is not always easy when seeking unique financing solutions. TBG's motto is "Making a Difference," and its team of loan advisors are dedicated to guiding clients in finding financing even in the most complex situations.

The Bradford Group Consulting (TBGC) is a business management consulting company that provides solution-oriented strategic planning and performance management support to profit, non-profit businesses, and government organizations both domestically and internationally. In addition to its strong business planning and analytical platform, TBGC offers customer and market analysis, board and executive management facilitation for governance and policies, organizational development and business management, and training and education. The Bradford Group Consulting is "making a difference one strategy at a time."

Conversation with LaWanna Bradford

Can you tell me how you got started as an entrepreneur?

LaWanna Bradford: It all started when I was in high school with my introduction to the Future Business Leaders of America program. I saw that there was so much opportunity in not only in owning a business, but in being a part of the economic engine that provides employment to others. That concept began to germinate within me and after college, I joined several multi-level marketing opportunities to practice my hands at business, particularly sales.

Soon after completing my master's degree in Administrative Organization and Management, I partnered with my current business partner, and we opened our first brick and mortar licensed sporting apparel store called Pro-Starter Sports, Inc. Our products included apparel, souvenirs, and equipment for both professional and collegiate levels. This frontline experience exposed me to all nuances and challenges of business from understanding how to negotiate leases, to doing building build outs, buying and pricing merchandise, and understanding the industry trends, developing marketing and advertising campaigns, and managing consumer demand. Pro Starter Sports, my first of several businesses that I built, gave me more experience than any book or any classroom could ever give, and it exponentially raised my business literacy. I think that is the time where I was infected with the entrepreneurial bug. I found myself fueled by living in the lanes of creativity and innovation.

Fast forward through the corporate world and retirement, I ultimately went into business management consulting. I joined my brother in the mortgage industry as a management consultant to facilitate the development of internal compliance guidelines and provide staff training. I soon realized that this was another industry where I could learn and grow, and I eagerly wanted to become a part of it. Long story short, I bought into the company; however, when the market started to spiral in 2007, my bother bailed, and I remained behind doing my best to tread water.

Needless to say, I survived the 2008 economic crisis and everything else is history. I think entrepreneurship is just a natural fit for me. Even in my professional life, I've always been in an internal consultant/advisory role, which continues to feed and foster that entrepreneurial bug of being creative and innovative and finding solutions. I consider myself a change agent, and all of my past experiences have shown me how my talents and knowledge can be used to help others create and sustain successful businesses.

Right now, we're in a time of economic challenges and economic opportunities for people during the COVID-19 pandemic. How do you see this unfolding?

LaWanna Bradford: Well, there are two lanes. You have those who are employed and those who are struggling financially due to loss of jobs or loss of business. Based on everything that we see, the projections look pretty bleak for the small and mid-sized businesses. Even big businesses aren't exempt. With the economy shut down and people's means to go out and buy goods and services and conduct commerce among themselves is compromised, it's going to have a crippling and long-term effect across the board.

Though individuals may not be directly impacted, there is an indirect economic ramification to what's happening. For those who are employed, they are still affected, but not as immediate. Right now, we are projected to be at 40 million unemployed. 40 million lost jobs, which will mean that all the gains that we made over the last 12-15 years will be washed away by the response to this pandemic.

One of the things that I tell individuals is that life happens because life is always going to happen. No job is everything. But you do have a creative genius that's within you. Therefore, you must ask yourself what can you do to market your skills, abilities in a unique way? Also, look at the resources that you have, and ask yourself:

How can you leverage those opportunities to help secure yourself in the future? It's about survival.

On the entrepreneurial side, there is a huge opportunity to do business differently because if you believe that how you did business a month ago is going to be the way you do business when we come out on the other side of COVID-19, you're grossly mistaken. So, I just encourage individuals to pay attention to the markets. Pay particular attention to your industry. What shifts are the major players making? Be ready to be in front in the wave. If you can't be in front of it, at least be willing to ride the crest of the wave, but don't stand and be overtaken by it.

With all of your experience, what would you say that your personal superpower is?

LaWanna Bradford: My superpower is I'm a strategist and an analyst, which means I'm watchful for the next critical move. I'm always positioning myself to find the opportunities, to find the steppingstones among the stumbling blocks. So, my superpower is I can assess the situation and predict what the next move may be and what my move should be. I'm able to work collaboratively with individuals to help them see the same thing. We hear the term "strategy" all the time, "Oh, let's be strategic in our thinking" But, that's not an innate skill. It requires ongoing application and refining your lens of how you look at life and how you look at business to truly elevate to strategic mastery.

I always caution individuals, when they say, "Oh, I'm joining this seminar, they're going to teach me strategies!" You don't learn strategy overnight. One key skillset is in understanding the environment that you're in. When you can really understand your industry and its contractions and expansions, then you sharpen your lens. This helps you to basically have that flashlight, if you will, to enable you to see how to navigate the landmines that are there. Right now, no matter what business you're in, there are a lot of landmines around us. So, it's about understanding the lay of the land, understanding your skillsets, your strengths, and then determining how you can navigate and forecast the next move and be in front of the play.

So, if your superpower is strategy, and in being able to forecast by looking at current events, do you have a suggestion for someone who finds themselves currently unemployed? Is this a good time to decide to do your own business? And, what should you be looking at to find out if it is for you?

LaWanna Bradford: I think the first thing is, if you find yourself in a place of being unemployed, or if you're a small business and because you've had to close your doors right now and your income stream has dried up, you have to first think about how are you going to eat. It's all about the basic necessities right now, keeping that roof over your head, feeding your family. Once you're able to meet your basic needs, then your mind is clearer. Then you can begin to be creative. I encourage individuals who are in that state, to question Where am I? What am I going to do? First, look at your finances. What reserves do you have? Do you have any? Now, look at how you're currently spending and where might you be able to reduce costs.

Since this is a federally mandated economic shutdown, there are so many programs that are out there, and private companies are partnering with the government to ensure that you don't lose your home. Contact your mortgage company if you own a home. What can you negotiate? Typically, they offer a 90-day deferment on your payments, so find out, would your interest go on the back end? You want to make sure you understand what that looks like for you. If you're a renter, based upon the guidelines, they should work with you and not evict you. You want to make sure you have those important conversations. What do you need to do to protect yourself from being put on out the streets? We're talking about survival right now.

The second thing is to find out if there are programs to help you if you need food supplies. I tell people, please put pride aside, many are in the same boat. You're not alone. So, it's okay. Also, if you have credit cards, the federal government has lowered the interest rate so either in your April or May statement, you should see a reduction there. However, if you find that you're unable to make that payment, talk to them. They have programs to assist. If you currently have car payments, they have options as well.

Instead of panicking, take the time and pull out your bills and see what must be paid immediately. See where you can cut costs and pick up the phone and have that real live dialogue. Work with your service providers and get yourself in the best position possible to ride out this wave.

If you want to think about starting your own business, now you will have the clarity of thought to be strategic and plan based upon your skills, talents and interests, rather than reacting and hoping that a shotgun approach is going to work.

In your journey, how have you promoted awareness and solutions to these types of issue that women and minority groups often face in the world today?

LaWanna Bradford: For the past eight months I've been on this the soapbox talking about the financial crisis facing women. Of course, this has been a long-time battle. When we think about women's push to get the right to vote, it was primarily seated on the concern of the inequities. If you look at the early 1900's, the same concerns we have today were the things that women were fighting for back then. When we're talking about parity, we must acknowledge that achieving equity is different for different groups. For example, pay equity for Caucasian women means that for the income that men earned in 2019, Caucasian women must work an extra four months to make what a white man earned. However, for African American women, they need to work an extra eight months to have the same level of pay. For Hispanic women, it's 11 months.

So, when you're looking at how long it's going to take for equity to be our reality, it will take 55 years for Caucasian women and almost 200 years for Hispanic women! It's so unfair, but what we as women must do across the board, not just in the U.S. but in all nations, is to continue to raise our voices and spotlight the issue. Then when we are in positions of leadership, we can hire ourselves and begin to tear down the walls of inequities. As I stated earlier, being an entrepreneur enables you to be an employer and by establishing those platforms and opening doorways will allow women to rise higher than they may have been able to in other male run companies.

The big word today is pivot. How does someone pivot their business? What have you had to do to pivot your business in 2020?

LaWanna Bradford: I don't typically use the term "pivot" because that means literally shifting and changing direction. From a strategic lens, if I have a goal, and if I turn directions, then the goal is actually behind me. So, the phrase that I use often is "repositioning to remain relevant." I'll share this very recent example. When the stimulus package came out, the Federal government adjusted the rates. Obviously, there was an impact on the mortgage side, and I thought, "Oh, great, now we're going to have lower interest rates, and we can help people move forward in their refinances and their purchases!" However, two weeks later, the market volatility just imploded, and it caused lenders to become very guarded and conservative in their lending.

What appeared to be an opportunity, now became a risk and a threat to our business. The lenders were, and they still are, looking at their portfolios, testing the qualifying guidelines, and making things more stringent. Why are they are doing that? Because they know that unemployment is going to rise, and they are afraid people are going to end up defaulting on their loans. So, they want to minimize their exposure even though they are being "bailed out" again. But because of this we are now assessing: What will this now mean to our business? So, where there was a potential opportunity, I now have 80% of my lenders saying, "Yeah, we'll still loan but we're going to loan at much higher interest rates." I'm not selling my clients that—that's just not how we do business.

Our motto is "making a difference," and we're now looking at different partner relationships to see how we might be able to provide our mortgage services. We may have to lean more on the commercial side than on the investor and homeowner side right now until things stabilize. This is an example of where we are repositioning to remain relevant. I believe if we, as a mortgage business, survived the biggest mortgage economic downturn in the history of the U.S. in 2007/2008, we will survive this. Today it's about pausing, being strategic and keeping that communication line open with our clients while informing and educating them. Because if I can't service you right now, from a product standpoint, I can service you by providing you with free education and knowledge so that you can protect your most precious asset which is your property.

As an educator and an advocate, what advice would you give an entrepreneur right now? What would you say would be the most important thing that they could be doing to be successful?

LaWanna Bradford: For me, success is giving your best in everything that you do. And when you do that, my dad would say, "Even the angels in Heaven couldn't ask more from you." So, give whatever you have in your ability and your capacity and you give it your all. When your heart is in it, it will give you heart-like rewards. I think that's what success is. I think it's when you put others before yourself and you position yourself as that person of service, whether in business and or in life.

As far as what an entrepreneur would absolutely need to be successful, I think the most important thing is vision. Without vision, you're not an entrepreneur, you've just created a job for yourself. You're a business owner. An entrepreneur is a visionary. That's a distinguishing difference. So, you must be able to have vision and that vision is ongoing. It's not a one and done. You're always in that creative genius mode. It's idea after idea after idea. Ideas are flowing. There are so many ideas with no time to do them all, but you're just keep writing them down. I think that having a vision is the fire that keeps entrepreneurs going, reinventing and recreating themselves.

How do you work with someone to help them create their strategic plan and implement it?

LaWanna Bradford: Most businesses, whether it's a big business or a small business, look at strategic planning as an exercise and as tangible end product. They create a strategic plan and it typically sits on the shelf and they'll dust it off the next year when it's the strategic planning cycle again, or maybe they'll look at it quarterly. But when I say it's an art, what makes it an art is that it becomes a part of you. It's in the way you look at the world. It becomes that creative lens. A true strategist is an artist, they have this blank canvas and are creating and dictating how the lay of the land will be— how this painting, or this tapestry, if you will, is going to be woven, because they're looking at the different parts that are impacting their business.

It's important to look at your dependencies, those things that you need to rely on in order to be successful. Look at your strategic partnerships and relationships, and understand your clients, not just who they are demographically, but how they operate and interact and think and make decisions. That's the psychographics, cost modeling, and processes within your business structure. So, imagine taking all these pieces and weaving them for the ultimate end that you want to get to.

Do you work with individuals?

LaWanna Bradford: I'm a consultant. I don't classify myself as a coach. From a strategy standpoint, as a consultant, I'm there to fill a gap that you may have in your business. If you don't have that strategic line of sight, then I will talk and work with individuals and ask them critical questions because what I'm trying to do is to have them turn on that switch of creative thinking. When you're able to start thinking creatively, that's the spark that ignites the genius of strategic thought. You have to get into that creative space first. In order to get creative, you must let all the noise, "all the ash and trash of life" go and get still and get quiet, and allow all the wild, crazy ideas to flow. You begin to move things around like pieces of a puzzle to see what fits and what doesn't. It's all about understanding timing, because you may have a great idea, but this is not the right time or place to execute. It doesn't mean that it goes away. You're just waiting for the right timing. And so, you still formulate it until it's ready and you're ready to execute.

I encourage both small and big businesses to first understand the landscape they're sitting in. When you understand that, then you've started to unpeel and unpack and remove the cloudiness of your own lens so that you're able to see much clearer. I've been to many small business sessions where they're teaching strategy and it's like, "Okay, let's come up with your goal. Let's decide on your timeline, and then your strategy…" and voila, you're done. Nine times out of 10, I can guarantee you will not achieve those goals because they are missing a critical, most important piece, and that's understanding the environment that you're in, and how all the nuances of it affect the goal. You need to determine your strengths and your weaknesses; those are the things you control and influence.

You must uncover what the opportunities and threats are and understand how those things that are outside of your control can impact you and your business negatively and/or positively. Discover how to leverage the opportunities and mitigate the threats. I try to help them understand it's not a "one and done." You don't take a class and instantly achieve strategic genius. I've been blessed where I've been doing it within many industries, from satellite communications to Olympic Committees to transportation to public health for over 30 years. My sight is very sharp and I'm able to simplify it for every type of industry. That's the brilliance of it, when you sharpen your strategic lens, you could do it in any lane all day long. I think that is going to be the difference in those who thrive on the other side of COVID-19 versus those who don't. Whether you have a cleaning service, or you're a big corporation, providing digital products, understanding the strategic landscape and having a strategic lens is key.

About LaWanna Bradford

Author LaWanna G. Bradford is a serial entrepreneur and global leader in the strategic planning and performance management arena. She is the COO of The Bradford Group, LLC, a commercial and investment mortgage brokerage and The Principal of The Bradford Group Consulting, LLC, a business management consulting firm. As a change agent, she leverages her 30+ years of experience working with federal and private industries to guide individuals toward achieving growth, understanding their market position, and increasing awareness of the customers they serve. She believes life should be embraced in the moment of now, and that positive transformation in life and in business is achieved one strategy at a time. Visit www.BradfordGroupMtg.com/about-us to learn more.

WEBSITE
BradfordGroupMtg.com

EMAIL
lawanna@bradfordgroupmtg.com

FACEBOOK
Facebook.com/LaWanna.Bradford.3

TWITTER
Twitter.com/LaWannaBradford

LINKEDIN
LinkedIn.com/in/LaWannaBradford

Barks & Berries: A Love Story

Jason Gardner created Barks & Berries to deliver the absolute best in fresh, natural, and wholesome dog nutrition. Barks & Berries started because his dog, Dobbie, had serious health issues – ones too early for her age. Dobbie suffered from liver problems and random infections that could never be traced to any one cause. Months were spent going from vet to vet with the hopes of discovering a cause and then finding a solution. Each veterinary visit meant new hope and came with new tests, but soon after yielded the same results. There was no diagnosable problem, but always a suggestion to alter Dobbie's diet and try new medications.

Each veterinarian recommended a different dog food and each new food brought a new reason as to why it was better and deemed "prescription only." However, something in each brand's ingredients stood out. Sugars and starches and additives were well hidden, but they were there. With an extensive background in human nutrition, endocrinology and human physiology, Jason could see something wasn't adding up. He knew that if he could identify ingredients that were essential and beneficial for a dog and eliminate anything that wasn't necessary, he could create something profoundly innovative and save Dobbie's life!

The result is a blend of thoroughly studied, wholesome ingredients with meticulously researched proportions to satisfy the biological needs of dogs while satisfying even the most discerning palates.

Within six months of starting her new diet, the long troublesome issues disappeared, and she went back to doing what she did best, being a healthy dog and a loving companion. Jason's pups have been eating this exclusively for more than six years with nothing to report but a pack of happy, healthy Papillons!

Conversation with Jason Gardner

Tell us more about Barks & Berries.

Jason Gardner: Barks & Berries is one of the first and only fresh organic dog food companies in the United States today. We are the only company that uses 100% whole food organic ingredients to provide and exceed all of the dietary nutrient requirements for dogs. No supplements, fillers, binding agents, or chemically processed ingredients that can take years off of your dog's life.

Why does no one ask why the life expectancy of humans has gone up over the last few decades, and yet the average life expectancy of most breeds of dogs in the U.S. is LOWER today than it was 40 years ago? We are proud to be an organization built around one mission. **To improve the lives of our pets through proper and advanced nutrition. We donate from each handcrafted batch of food we make to local rescues, so that all dogs get the nutrition they need in the most stressful times of their lives. We won't stop growing until fresh food becomes the norm for all dogs everywhere.**

Why did you start Barks & Berries?

Jason Gardner: I have a puppy, Dobbie, and she got really sick. So, I decided to do what I could to make her feel better. We had a lot of years of being in and out of the vet. Finally, at the end of all that, I had a couple of different vets tell me it was time to put her down and she was only six years old. At that point, her medical issues had been going on since she was four. I just decided I wasn't going to give up, so I decided I would use my entire background— 20 plus years—studying human nutrition, physiology, endocrinology to find an answer for Dobbie. I started researching dog nutrition, canine physiology, and learning everything that I could about that. You quickly realize when you start to research canine nutrition, that for all the differences there are between types of dog food, there are also a lot of similarities in the foods that we have available. And, a lot of the foods that are good for humans do great things for dogs, too. Dobbie is sitting on the floor at my feet right now, happy and healthy.

Why is she so healthy now? What did you find out about dog nutrition that literally saved your little dog's life?

Jason Gardner: Dobbie was the first dog that I ever had, I got another one two years into having her to keep her company but, there's a special bond that you get with your first dog. It's just you and the dog and you're doing everything together. When she got sick, and when all of this happened, and the vet started saying, "You're just going have to put her down. She's not going have any quality of life." It tore me up. I was trying everything I could while I was also researching everything about how to help her. They diagnosed her with everything from Cushing's to chronic liver and kidney infections and enlargement of the heart. They said she had arthritis, at only four years old.

I would take her in because she would be vomiting, we would go to the vet, they would run their blood test, treat the vomiting and find out that that was a stomach infection and then as we treated the stomach infection, I would take her home for two weeks and find her entire abdomen was discolored and purple and not obviously not right. So, I would take her back in and then we would find out that her kidneys were failing, and she wasn't processing things and then it was a liver infection. This was just a cycle for years and years, steroids and anti-inflammatories and this prescription diet or that prescription diet and nothing helped.

When we got the recommendation to put her down, I was kind of lost for a little bit. I started researching as much as I could about canine physiology and nutrition and what caused all these things. What we later found out was that it was all caused by a massive immunodeficiency, but through two years of bloodwork and everything else, nobody could tell me that. That really bothered me.

It also made me realize that, just changing Dobbie's diet, adding in whole foods, organic foods, nothing processed, none of these weird filler supplements that all these companies use, so that I knew exactly what she was getting could control how much calcium she got, and using a natural form of calcium and everything else we were able to heal her within three months. This is a dog that didn't have normal blood work for two and a half years, was healed in three months through changing her diet alone. I took her in to the vet after three months of taking her off all the prescription food, all the medications, everything, and just feeding her the whole, healthy, organic foods and her blood work was normal for the first time in two and a half years.

What are the main mistakes that most people make when choosing dog food?

Jason Gardner: Sadly, it's the same mistakes a lot of people make in choosing their own food. The biggest one is not doing research. Not reading the labels. Even for the people who do read the labels, the majority of them will gloss over the things if they don't know what they are. When you start getting to the bottom half of a dog food label, especially for processed foods, most people don't even know what those ingredients are or what they mean. I didn't know either when I first became a dog owner. As I learned about the chemicals that manufacturers are adding into the foods and artificial preservatives and things that are toxic to humans, it just didn't make sense to me. It didn't add up.

I would say the first mistake is not reading the food labels and not understanding what those ingredients are. Then, going a little bit deeper than that, not understanding the dog food industry. The industry as a whole is owned by three companies. They have over 86% of the market share of dog food. These companies are using rancid meats and diseased animals. It doesn't have to be clean. It can be sitting out in the sun for days before you process it and put it in animal food. We would never put that stuff in our bodies. Even though there's an argument saying that since dogs are descended from wolves, it shouldn't matter: it does. Today's dogs that are pets are many generations removed from wolves. My Dobbie has nothing in common with a wolf. Her digestive system, her internal flora, her microbiome, is not of a wolf. She was not meant to eat diseased old animal carcasses. It's developed over time. When people don't understand that, and they don't go research those things, they allow a massive misinformation campaign from these major dog food companies to let them poison their pets. The average lifespan of Golden retrievers back in the 1970s was 14 to 17 years old and now, for that same dog breed the average lifespan is 10 to 14. And, we're spending three times as much money at the vet to make them live three quarters of the lifespan that they used to live. It just doesn't make sense.

Most people only consider the price of dog food. One thing that really makes Barks & Berries different is the fact that it's organic. What should people be looking for in a good dog food?

Jason Gardner: The biggest is to ignore the marketing gimmicks there are out there. Things like how the food is a "limited ingredient" food. Well, offering your dog a "limited ingredient food" doesn't make any sense. As humans, we don't eat the same five foods every day all day, and then supplement the other 50% of the nutrients that we need artificially, and dogs shouldn't either. When I was creating the Barks & Berries, I wanted none of that. In our dog food recipes, we have more than 45 whole food ingredients. We don't use any supplements to meet all of the nutritional requirements for dogs. Everything comes from whole foods. Because it comes from whole foods, their bodies are able to get the nutrients in the form that it was designed to be delivered to them. It has the most bioavailability. Their bodies absorb the nutrients the way they're supposed to absorb them. They're getting them in the forms that they're supposed to which helps them live their healthiest life.

I would say the biggest difference in Barks & Berries, other than the fact that it's all organic grass-fed meat, is that we use nothing but whole food ingredients. We're the only dog food company out there that can make that claim. Every other dog food company, including the fresh food companies, use a proprietary supplement blend along with their five to 10 ingredients to get those nutritional needs up to where they are. And unfortunately, those supplement blends are not controlled by those companies. They're usually outsourced by third parties, and they have all kinds of fillers. Some of them have preservatives in them. You have these "fresh" dog food companies that are advertising no preservatives added, but the preservatives are coming in the form of their proprietary supplement blends that they don't release. At Barks & Berries, we don't have any of that—everything is made from whole food. Everything is organic. Everything is grass fed and it's locally sourced.

How are you able to source everything locally, and what exactly does that mean?

Jason Gardner: We work with more than 25 different local farms, ranches, and individuals who grow or raise all of our ingredients for us. It's a beautiful thing to me because I can, at any point in time, show up to any of these farms or ranches and see the conditions that the animals are being raised in, the conditions that the produce is being grown in and the conditions that our herbs and things that we use are being grown in. That means a lot to me because, for me, I want to know what I'm feeding my pet is the best.

Starting this company has changed my own eating habits a lot even though my background was human nutrition to begin with. We don't really pay attention to where things come from. Sourcing, especially now with FDA labeling changes on the foods that we eat and buy at the grocery store is one of the most muddled, hard things to find. I want to know—where are these meats are coming from? A lot of them are going to other countries and coming back or starting in other countries where the growing standards and the standards of raising them, administering antibiotics and growth hormones and things like that are not regulated like they are here.

So, when you buy things like that, you're running a huge risk that you don't really know how those things were raised. You don't know what pesticides were sprayed on the fruits and veggies; you don't know what hormones were injected into the meats. And, again, I didn't want anything to do with that. Everything we source is local. I have some great relationships with the people that we work with and I'm always looking for new sources for things. For the first time we might not go local for one of our ingredients, and that's going to be our lamb dog food recipe, which is going to be a new one. We have a great resource for getting New Zealand lamb, and we can track all the way back to each individual ranch and land where the lambs were raised, so that's pretty exciting.

How did you come up with the recipes that you have and how many recipes do you have?

Jason Gardner: Right now, we have two recipes for the dog nutrition products. We have dog treats and other things too, but in the beginning, basically I was looking for what the needs are for canine physiology for all the different macro and micronutrients, probiotics, enzymes, proteins, carbs, fats, vitamins and minerals and then put together a recipe that would get the exact right levels of all of those things. In the early days, I showed a friend who is a holistic veterinarian my recipe and her response was, "This is the healthiest food I've ever seen!" That's was the validation that I needed to start Dobbie on it. From there, what it's done for hundreds and thousands of other dogs over the last several years is just amazing. Every time somebody tells me that their dog wasn't eating and wasn't able to stand up or move around and now it's acting like it was at two years old again, that just makes me feel great.

Let's talk about the special ingredients in your Barks & Berries dog food recipes. Mushrooms are supposed to be really good for you—and apparently, they are really good for dogs too. You have something called the "magic mushroom" mix. What is that?

Jason Gardner: The magic mushroom mix is probably one of the things I'm most proud of. I've done research into mushrooms for a long time because, especially in Eastern medicine, they have so many uses—from being anti-inflammatory and creating energy to improving circulation and brain function. One of the biggest benefits is the research on their potential for anti-tumor and anti-cancer effects. If you research all the different types of mushrooms and their benefits for dogs, there's five that top the list for anti-cancer effects in dogs, but also many other things from anti-inflammatory to anti-microbial and anti-bacterial. The "magic mushroom mix" is six different kinds of mushrooms. They're all organic, it's a powder that you can sprinkle on top of their food or mix with their food. It's included already in our treat recipes and our dog food itself. But people who just want to use it as a topper or when have sick dogs and they want to add a little bit more they can use that mix. We use medicinal mushrooms like Chaga, Turkey tail, Lion's mane, Reishi and Cordyceps. It's a phenomenal supplement, especially for older dogs, sick dogs, and just as a preventative.

You advise not to microwave the food. Why is that?

Jason Gardner: Our food is all fresh food. All of our ingredients are from whole food sources, which means they have active enzymes. They have live probiotics, pre-biotics, and they have all of these live active cultures in them. When you microwave something, you kill off all of that instantly. If you buy, organic whole food, like the Barks & Berries food, and then you throw it in the microwave, you're essentially killing off 80% of the good stuff that's in it. So, microwaving is a big no-no.

Are you planning on expanding Barks & Berries into any retail stores?

Jason Gardner: Originally, it was going to be a subscription-based service where people could sign up their dog for the food and anything else that they needed, and it would be delivered to their door so it's something that they don't have to worry about. Over time, I realized that a lot of people still want to be able to go into a pet store. Just within the last 30 days, I've been approached by two major retailers in the US and Canada about putting my food in the retail store. So, there is a good chance that within the next three to six months, you'll see Barks & Berries in the retail store.

Do you have any new products coming up that you haven't let out yet?

Jason Gardner: Our whole treat line is actually pretty new. We're constantly coming up with new flavors for our treats. We have three permanent flavors right now and then one that is seasonal. The treats, just like our food, are all organic, and they all have a reason for every ingredient that's in them. These dog treats are made from lamb, or liver—all these good things—but they don't have any of the junky white flour or any of the other stuff that you'll see in other types of dog treats. These have our mushroom powder too. We also have a new powder that's coming out. It's our super antioxidant blend—with things like Maca, Spirulina, Goji berry and Acai berry. So that's an antioxidant powder that will be another topper to boost up antioxidants. We have that in some of our recipes for treats now. The treats have fresh herbs baked right into them, so they're getting all the benefits of those as well. Other than the seasonal treats and the new super antioxidant blend that we have coming out, we have a cat food line that's being researched right now! So that'll be something that you'll see over the next probably three to six months too!

Barks & Berries started out being for dogs, and soon there will be a new line for cats. Do you foresee that you might also move into human food?

Jason Gardner: No. People can make their own choices about what types of foods and ingredients they will eat, but dogs can't. You have to make those choices for them. Our niche is taking care of the animals and making sure that we maintain the best dog food on the market for as long as possible.

Can you tell me about your program to assist shelter pets?

Jason Gardner: I do everything that I can to help rescues and pet shelters, it is a passion of mine. When all the COVID-19 stuff started, a lot of people were really scared. Unfortunately, what that meant was people were turning in their pets to rescues and shelters and rescues and shelters were shutting down because they didn't have people that could come in. It became a big issue for a lot of these great people who are trying to help dogs. I knew that we had to do something. So, we put our "Keep the Pets Fed" initiative together. We started donating 50% of all of our sales to feed the dogs at rescues and shelters. We were interviewed on (Phoenix) Fox 10 news about the "Keep the Pets Fed" initiative. That's something that we're doing through the end of May 2020.

If people want to donate, 100% of those donations go to food for rescues and shelters and anybody that orders through the end of May 2020, we're taking the value of that order and donating that as well in food back to the rescues and shelters. I feel like we've done a lot of good for a lot of the local rescues out here.

If you really care about your dog, take a good hard look at what you're feeding them. Extra vet visits and medical bills and the shortened lifespans are things that we can change if we just take a little bit of time and are willing to invest a little bit more of our resources whether that's time or money into giving them the good nutrition that they need. We can add years to their lives, and we can add health and vitality and fun to those years.

Do you ship outside of the Phoenix area where you are based?

Jason Gardner: We ship all over the US. The only place we don't ship is Alaska and Hawaii. We ship all of our orders for free. You can go on our website; we actually have some sampler packs coming soon so people can try a little bit of everything first and see which recipe their dogs prefer.

As business owners, we're often told how great it is to pursue your passion when you start a business–but we've spoken with enough people to know that it's not always easy. Overall, would you say things have been easy for you starting Barks & Berries?

Jason Gardner: Our path to creating Barks & Berries may not have been smooth at times, but it's always been straight. Obstacles come up and can derail a weak vision pretty quickly. We've known from day one the fight we were walking into with major corporations—we knew we'd be fighting to stay relevant in a trillion-dollar industry. I walk the path to do the right thing and prepare to get bloody doing it. Pet food is overregulated and under researched. Most veterinarians don't know the first thing about pet food. Of the brilliant ones who do – and often champion our causes – they face professional criticisms and backlash regularly. We've been fortunate to work with some amazing holistic veterinary nutritionists and see firsthand the fight they fight to keep our pets safe from an industry dominated by corruption and greed at the expense of our precious pets.

We've faced challenges with sourcing sustainable, quality organic ingredients as well as scaling growth to handle the demand for our food. All of these challenges have been overcome through an amazing network of passionate friends, business owners, communities and pet health advocates that have been there at every turn to help us carry on and grow.

Has luck played a meaningful role in your life and business?

Jason Gardner: I think luck plays a role in everything. In life and business, I've had my fair share of both. I enjoy the times that come with good luck. Be it the people or events God put in my life at that time to make things easier, I've always tried to be appreciative of where I am and where I've been. The bad luck is where the growth comes from, and when the hard work becomes necessary. It shows you what you're capable of and tests your resolve in making your dreams a reality. Overall, I've been fortunate, even though there's been bad times, myself and the people around me, friends, family and colleagues have always fought the hard fight to get through to the other side. Surround yourself with the right people, and they'll get you through the hard times.

If somebody wants to reach out, what's the best way for them to contact you?

Jason Gardner: Visit our website BarksAndBerries.com. You can reach out to us via email at info@barksandberries.com. If you have questions, send them on Facebook or Instagram.

About Jason Gardner

Jason Gardner started Barks & Berries in 2016. After feeding this formula to his own dogs for almost 10 years, he has seen a huge improvement in their health, especially Dobbie, who as she grew older, started displaying some serious health issues – ones too early for her age. Dobbie suffered from liver problems and random infections that could never be traced to any one cause. Months were spent going from vet to vet with the hopes of discovering a cause and then finding a solution. Each veterinary visit meant new hope and came with new tests, but soon after yielded the same results. There was no diagnosable problem but always a suggestion to alter Dobbie's diet. Something in each brand's ingredients stood out. Sugars and starches and additives were well hidden, but they were there.

With an extensive background in human nutrition, endocrinology and human physiology, Jason could see something wasn't adding up. He knew that if he could identify ingredients that are essential and beneficial for a dog and eliminate anything that wasn't necessary, Jason could create something profoundly innovative and save his poor girl's life! The quest began and it started with months of research, endless consultations with leading veterinary nutritionists and veterinarians, and the careful study of existing dog food ingredients and how they impact canine physiology.

Research and perseverance crafted an exclusive list of ingredients that made sure to include the nutrients that Dobbie desperately needed from whole food sources and not chemically refined and processed supplements, while eliminating non-essential and toxic ones. The result is a blend of thoroughly studied, wholesome ingredients with meticulously researched proportions to satisfy the biological needs of dogs while satisfying even the most discerning palates. It's not dog food. It is better than that…it is dog nutrition!

WEBSITE
BarksAndBerries.com

EMAIL
info@barksandberries.com

FACEBOOK
Facebook.com/BarksandBerries

INSTAGRAM
Instagram.com/BarksAndBerries

The Art of Jazz

Donna Singer has returned from Paris and singing at Carnegie Hall. Her European tour to Switzerland and in Italy was a huge success. Her tour finale took place in New York City with a performance at the Metropolitan Opera Guild Recital Hall in Lincoln Center, and Central Park's Naumburg Bandshell. Donna is a graduate of the New York Academy of the Theatrical Arts with formal training at The Juilliard School. She was honored by the Jazz Radio Show *Straight No Chaser,* as the "Singer of the Year," backed by *The Doug Richards Trio*, for the "Kiss Me Beneath the Mistletoe" CD last year. She sang the national anthem for a Miami Dolphins game, and she's headlined at the Bethany Jazz Concert in Kansas, the Nebraska International Jazz Festival, the Saratoga Arts Festival, the Newburgh Jazz Series, and the New York Heritage Festival, as well as at the amphitheater in Vienna, Virginia. Donna Singer's newest album, "Set Your Heart Free" is available worldwide as of June 5, 2020.

Conversation with Donna Singer

How did you get involved with jazz?

Donna Singer: I grew up in a very, very strong jazz family. My parents were not professional musicians, but they loved listening to jazz and dancing. My mother had a wonderful voice and would sing along to jazz records every night after we went to bed. Sunday afternoons were the days my dad would play instrumental jazz. Not only did we grow up listening to John Coltrane, Miles Davis, Oscar Peterson and so many others, we were also listening to jazz vocal artists like, Sarah Vaughan, Ella Fitzgerald, Billie Holiday, Nancy Wilson, Anita O'Day, and my personal favorite, Dinah Washington. We were just listening to these albums and all of a sudden, I started singing them on a regular basis—just in our basement and in our family room. I started singing them and my mom would say I was singing or humming nursery rhymes at a very young age. So, I've been singing a long time. My father introduced me to all of these wonderful women and men, Johnny Hartmen, Sammy Davis, Jr, Nat King Cole. They resonated with me at a very early age. I was singing "Mr. Paganini" and "What a Difference a Day Made" and it stuck.

So, you started singing when you were little? Did you follow your musical dreams with formal music education?

Donna Singer: I did all the school musicals, sang in chorus and performed at my high school graduation and then, when I went off to college, I majored in Theater Education at The New York Academy of Theatrical Arts. I remember my audition because the professors didn't say a word to me. I thought, "Well, what kind of audition is this?" I sang a song from *A Chorus Line* and they didn't say a word! Needless to say, I did get in! So strange and funny!

You went to The Juilliard School later on?

Donna Singer: I went to The Juilliard School in New York City as an adult. After I had graduated from the Academy, I faced the real world and took a job. I really put music in the background career-wise. Then I auditioned for Juilliard as an adult. I got into their night program and studied. I just said, "This is what I want to do".

I started performing with my husband, Roy. I met him the year before I auditioned for Juilliard and his last name is Singer. Roy Singer. So, that's my real name, not a stage name. Roy's from Kansas and he's a composer who studied at the Philadelphia Musical Academy. Roy really encouraged me to audition for Juilliard.

Do you have any recollection of any concerts that you went to when you were a kid?

Donna Singer: I went to two major concerts when I was a kid that I remember clearly. I went to a Commodores concert in the late 70's and it was just phenomenal. The energy, the excitement, the singing and dancing to all those great songs really resonated with me. That feeling in the audience that we were all a part of something special and amazing. I saw what it took to be, not just a performer, but also an entertainer! You've got to be technically great and you also have to give the audience a great time! Something I've never forgotten.

I got the Broadway bug when our parents took us to see *The Wiz* with Stephanie Mills! Wow! Being a part of that audience, I began to imagine myself on that stage and capturing a crowd and making them want to stay to the end of the story. It was an unforgettable experience. I will also add that I got the opportunity to go to the Jackson Five reunion tour in 1983 and no one had more showmanship than the Jackson Five! Incredible! I wanted to be on stage; I wanted to be a performer; I wanted to be an entertainer! I wanted to sing!

You have been around the world singing jazz. Do you have a favorite performance?

Donna Singer: I love singing in front of large audiences. I was blessed to sing at 'Jazz in June', the Nebraska International Jazz Festival at Lincoln University. There were almost 6000 people there and a phenomenal electricity in the air. You could just feel it, we were all into it. We were all having a great time. However, my favorite performances I recall were singing in small nightclubs down in Greenwich Village in New York City.

It was just me and the piano and you in the third row. I really enjoyed connecting with that one person in the audience who is really having a good time! You feel that energy, but it is also such an intimate experience. You get to really engage with your audience and get to know people and give them what they want. I will always have a soft spot for the small clubs and love going to as many as I can in whatever city I happen to be visiting.

You were also an "Artist in Residence" in Switzerland – what does that mean?

Donna Singer: Yes, I was an "Artist in Residence" I was invited to study for three weeks, immerse myself in the local culture, rehearse and create, teach master classes, and present a festival performance at the end of my time there. We stayed in a beautiful white chalet in the Swiss Alps. It was an amazing three weeks! They advertised that if anybody wanted to come and have a free vocal lesson, we've got Donna Singer! So, whatever singing level you were or whatever your singing style was, I would be available to train and consult. Then we did a show at the end of those three weeks.

They were so kind. They asked me if I would be willing to do a few local shows and I said "of course!" I love studying my art, but the reality is I always want to perform. As I had my trio with me, we ended up doing seven shows in Switzerland. We even found some time to go over the border to Italy and did a show there. It was phenomenal. The whole experience was great.

Did you bring your trio with you?

Donna Singer: Yes, I brought my trio with me to Europe. My husband, Roy Singer was our pianist, Hunter Isbell of Delray Beach, FL was on bass and William Fleck, of Mountaindale, NY was on trombone. The majority of our shows were small and intimate – one show was in someone's living room! It was great. Being an "Artist in Residence" worked out well because we could also work on new material. My material is very extensive. I'm very fortunate. Not only do I do the great music of Ella Fitzgerald, and Sarah Vaughan, I've also incorporated Tina Turner and Diana Ross. I was able to bring in artists from another generation in a jazz flavor, and still have fun with it.

You recently moved to South Florida from the Catskills in New York?

Donna Singer: Yes, we did! Roy and I decided to hit the sunshine state. The Catskills are an hour and a half from New York City so, I was fortunate to perform jazz clubs in the Catskills and in New York City. Now I've moved to South Florida and have been experiencing an entirely new jazz scene that is extensive and exciting.

You work with The Doug Richards Trio and have made five albums?

Donna Singer: I met Doug at a small gig, and he played electric bass, not upright bass. I've never heard the bass guitar so strong and so perfect in a jazz trio. Doug played with Erskine Hawkins of Tuxedo Junction fame. He also played in bands that featured Frank Sinatra and Sammy Davis, Jr. He played with all the greats. He was one of the musicians who lived in the Catskill Mountains during its heyday of the 60's. So, I just happened to hear him, and I struck up a conversation with him and he says, "Why don't you come sing a song up on stage?" And I said, "Yeah, I think I will." So, I sang "Bye Bye Blackbird" made popular by Sammy Davis, Jr. and the rest was history. He brought his trio into the studio and we made our first album *"Jazz In The Living Room."* We made six albums in all.

1) *Jazz In The Living Room*
2) *Take The Day Off: Escape With Jazz*
3) *Kiss Me Beneath the Mistletoe*
4) *Destiny Moment of Jazz*
5) *It's An Art To Follow Your Heart*
6) *Feeling The Jazz*

They are played on five continents and have charted in the 20's on the NACC Charts (NPR and College Radio) and Roots Music Report. I enjoyed my tenure with The Doug Richards Trio. Billy Alfred on piano who was the musical director at the Pines Hotel for 25 years and Mike Cervone on drums who is now with Jazzmosis in Upstate New York. Doug passed away a few years back and I treasure our moments. I'll always feel privileged for the opportunity to create wonderful music with Doug Richards and his fabulous trio. I now work with Brad Keller, piano, Ranses Colon, bass, Adolfo Herrera, drums. I'm looking forward to continued success with my new trio.

Speaking of this new album, what is it?

Donna Singer: My 7th album is called, *"Set Your Heart Free,"* The best way to describe it is, we all have a road we travel from childhood to adulthood. We experience glorious highs and the emotional lows on this journey. The magnificent songs of this album, which are all original, reflect the childhood days *"When You Have a Dream"* to young adulthood when you *"Spread Your Wings"* to finally finding *"Your Road"* to a brighter future.

This album's repertoire is remarkable, as most of the pieces are written by the award winning, accomplished team of Mitchell Uscher and Roy Singer. These two composers have varied backgrounds making them a complementary pair. Bringing the compositions to life is the all-star band: Brad Keller (piano), Ranses Colon (bass), Adolfo Herrera (drums), Melton Mustafa Jr. (saxophones), Yamin Mustafa (trumpet), and Greg Minnick (guitar). The superb mix and master is by veteran Grammy winner Antonio (Tony) Tahan.

What are the new songs? Are you a composer?

Donna Singer: No, I am not a composer, but I am working with some really amazing composers and musicians for this album. There are 10 original songs on this new album. Three were composed by the wonderful Oren Levine based out of Washington, DC. He has such a way with lyrics and melodies that I feel so privileged to be singing them. His songs touch on the feelings and emotions of growing up and learning that life has highs and lows, as well as how to keep moving forward. My husband, Roy Singer is a masterful composer and he and his writing partner, Mitchell Uscher wrote five songs for me. He knows my style and he knows what will make people come back to a song over and over again. Their songs are inspirational and up-lifting. The last song was written by my good friend, the world-renowned artist, Hope London based in Scotland. In addition to her gift for painting and all things art, she writes poetry and amazing songs. Her song, *"To be a Child?"* gives us all something to think about.

When does this CD come out?

Donna Singer: The CD came out June 5, 2020. It is available online on iTunes, Spotify, Pandora, Amazon and more. Review copies were out on May 1, 2020, which means the magazines get 20 to 30 days to review the CD before it hits the street.

In New York City, like you said, they have jazz clubs and a large music scene. How has moving to South Florida affected your musical life?

Donna Singer: Moving to Florida has been fantastic. I have hooked up with some great musicians. I met many by just going to clubs and going to hear jazz throughout the area in Fort Lauderdale, Miami and West Palm Beach. I sing with my18-piece Diamond Jazz Orchestra. Also, with the 80-member Gold Coast Concert Band and various Jazz Trios and Quartets.

Has COVID-19 affected some of your dates and shows?

Donna Singer: All of my dates were cancelled as of February 2020 when the COVID-19 virus became widespread. I had performances scheduled in Phoenix, New York City and Scandinavia. We were to go to Denmark, Sweden, Finland, and Norway. They were cancelled for 2020.

I've started booking performances for 2021 and we're going to go back to New York, performing at Alvin Ailey American Dance Theater. As well as adding performances from Vienna to Prague on a cruise of The Danube River. In 2022, I will be on my rescheduled Scandinavia Tour. So I'm excited that things are picking up. It has been sad not being able to perform live, but it's given me time to focus on my CD. I just pray that people are safe. When the time is right, we will be back!

Some performers are singing and having paid concerts on Facebook Live. Do you have any plans on maybe getting together with your trio somehow and doing any type of concert online?

Donna Singer: I'm going to be honest with you, I have not really focused on Facebook concerts because *"Set Your Heart Free"* has taken up much of my time and I want it to be the best it can be. The pandemic has impacted the world in so many different ways and at this time, I honestly don't have the energy to do more right now. I will say that I am enjoying immensely what these artists are doing online. The music is phenomenal!

Can your fans help you win a Grammy award? Or, is that an industry award?

Donna Singer: This is a Yes/No question. Technically, fans can help a CD or artist win a Grammy by helping its popularity. The Recording Academy is a closed group that does pay attention to what the fans are listening to. So, the more you support your artist by buying and listening to songs the more I have a chance to win. I can vote because I'm a voting member of The Recording Academy, but only members can vote.

Also, fans help tremendously through the Nielsen ratings. If you buy even one song that goes to the Nielsen ratings and if I'm on the Billboard charts, that obviously gets my name out there. If you can get your name out there, The Recording Academy members will remember. If they've never heard of Donna Singer, why should they vote for her music? It's really that simple. We're telling all of our fans and all of our friends to spread the word.

How can fans buy and share your music?

Donna Singer: Yes! Please buy my music and share! But seriously, whether you buy my music or listen to songs for free on my website, I will know you love me and my music! This is all about the love of jazz and if you love jazz, you'll want to hear it as much as you can. You can find me on my website Donna-Singer.com and all social media platforms.

My music is for my fans and will always reflect what they are looking for in jazz now and in the future.

About Donna Singer

Powerhouse performer Donna Singer has wowed jazz lovers around the world through her recordings and live performances at festivals, concert halls and jazz clubs. Her European concerts include dates in Paris, Switzerland, Ireland, Italy and Wales. She has performed at Carnegie Hall, The Metropolitan Opera Guild Recital Hall in Lincoln Center, Central Park's Naumburg Bandshell in New York City and The Kravis Center for the Performing Arts in West Palm Beach.

She has engaged audiences in many U.S. cities including Miami, Phoenix, and Nashville. Her U.S. festival appearances include the Nebraska International Jazz Festival, Bethany College Jazz Festival in Kansas and the Saratoga Arts Festival in New York. Whether performing in an intimate gathering with her trio, with an 18-piece jazz orchestra, or with the 90-piece Boynton Beach Gold Coast Band, she is sure to wow.

Growing up in Upstate New York, she and her siblings were introduced to the world of jazz. She and her twin sister, Dawn, were raised in a family of jazz enthusiasts who listened to the music of great jazz artists like Nancy Wilson ("Guess Who I Saw Today,") Billy Strayhorn, ("Take the A Train" with Duke Ellington), Sammy Davis, Jr., ("Hey There," and Count Basie ("April in Paris").

Donna's voice is showcased on seven recordings which have consistently climbed high in U.S. radio charts. Her music is heard on the playlists of hundreds of radio stations worldwide, as well as on Internet stations. She has also enjoyed international airplay. Donna's CD's are available on all major music outlets and her YouTube videos have been seen by over half a million viewers. In 2011, she became a recording executive, creating her own label, Emerald Baby Recording Company. Donna looks forward to spreading her love of jazz for many years to come and hmmm, Christmas album anyone?

"Donna Singer is a first call vocalist...with an effervescent spirit and impeccable phrasing there is certainly no lack of talent."

– Brent Black, @Critical Jazz

WEBSITE
Donna-Singer.com

EMAIL
jazz@donna-singer.com

FACEBOOK
Facebook.com/Donna.Singer.7370

TWITTER
Twitter.com/DrDonnaSinger1

INSTAGRAM
Instagram.com/DrDonnaSinger

PINTEREST
Pinterest.com/DrDonnaSinger

LINKEDIN
LinkedIn.com/in/Dr-Donna-Singer-a44b43a

YOUTUBE
YouTube.com/user/DrDonnaSinger1

How Implementing Systems Improves Productivity and Profitability for Small Business Owners

Claire E. Jones offers systematized business solutions to arts organizations and small businesses so that they can grow and scale their businesses without burning out. There's a ton of business advice and information out there, but people are often overwhelmed and overworked so they don't know where to start.

After working with arts organizations and small businesses for 15 years, Claire has the experience to see the trends and themes across the board that can make or break a small business's ability to grow and scale. She has created a consulting system that focuses on three pillars of business success as a way to focus her clients and help them create targeted holistic fixes for their businesses.

Conversation with Claire E. Jones

What problems do you help businesses solve?

Claire E. Jones: I help businesses put adequate systems in place because many people build businesses off of their passions without really knowing what it takes to run a business. One of my core values is freedom of self-expression. I believe that many small business owners and organizations build their businesses out of self-expression and passion, so they want to work in that zone of genius *and* have a thriving, profitable business. Being prepared with the knowledge, experience or skill sets required to run a successful business is something they struggle with because they are trying to do everything themselves.

I work with my clients to put systems in place so they can have more time for that zone of genius or whatever they want to have more time for, whether it's family, friends, or vacations. Many small business owners don't feel like they can take time for themselves, but with proper systems in place, they'll be able to grow and scale sustainably without constantly reinventing the wheel. The result is they are happier, more productive, and more strategic overall.

I also help my clients avoid the temptation to DIY everything because eventually everyone gets to the point where they hit their limit. So, either they don't have sufficient knowledge or experience to do it themselves or they don't have sufficient time, energy or motivation to learn how to do it. It's difficult to scale that way. They might even hire the first person who comes along or buy the first software program that promises to fix their problem without taking the time to research or compare costs. This can lead to being stuck with a patchwork business that you just hope and pray works well together. So, I come in say, "All right, these are the options available to us, and this is the recommended strategy that we need to implement to save time, money, and energy down the road."

How do you assess the systems they may need to implement?

Claire E. Jones: I look at the big picture of their business and make sure that all of the systems and processes they're using are appropriate and are producing positive R.O.I. This includes schedules and making sure that they're prioritizing their time correctly, ensure the marketing strategies and marketing efforts are giving them quality ROI, and making sure that the software, applications, and strategies they are using on a daily basis to run their business work together. All of these come together to create a well-oiled machine rather than a patchwork of DIY fixes.

I help them get more done in less time so that their time is streamlined and they don't continually run into the same obstacles.

Can you give an example?

Claire E. Jones: One of my current clients is launching her company nationally. She's been working in the local area for about 10 years, but she's ready for a broader audience. One of the problems she is facing is that all of her marketing strategies and systems are outdated and not ready for a national audience. They're not cohesive or consistent because as she went along, she was like, Oh, I need a Facebook page, so I'll put together a Facebook page. Oh, I need this. I'll put it together something... all without having that overarching big picture strategy in place.

As I started working with her, one of her big problems was her website because when it was originally built, it was built entirely via code without a content management system in place for easy updates and postings she could do herself. Now, it has outdated information an pictures. She knew it was time to update and was considering hiring the web designer that had implemented the last updates for her, but that would have cost thousands of dollars and she still wouldn't be able to make future updates without paying loads of money to that web designer.

I showed her a better route and helped her find a developer who would give her an 18-month contract that charged significantly less than the one-time upfront payment required by the previous designer. Plus, any updates that she needed during that 18-month contract would be done at no additional cost, and they would even train her on the new WordPress-based website. Now, she has all of the proper systems in place to scale and grow without having to reinvent the wheel every single time.

If my clients are looking for a social media manager, they need to know what social media specifically does for their business to pick the right person to do it. It's the same with the website development. They need to know fundamentally what a website does, how to access it and how it works so that they can more thoroughly and comprehensively vet the people they're hiring to do those tasks down the road. I very much emphasize education and empowering my clients to make those decisions in an educated way.

What are some common misconceptions you see?

Claire E. Jones: One of the biggest misconceptions that I see is that business owners and business builders need to work harder to get to the next level of success. It's very common for people to disregard their own needs, their health or their personal development because they think they need to put all of that energy and intention into the business. The sustainability of the business depends directly on the people who are running it and their own personal sustainability. You can only develop a business as far as you are willing and able to develop yourself. I often see people not scheduling enough time for themselves in their daily routines to bring their best selves to the business. That's when they get overworked and overwhelmed because they don't prioritize their time well in a way that allows them to perform better.

Another pitfall that I often see people falling into is hiring the wrong person once they realize that they need to delegate. When they do delegate or do hire, they will pick the first person that comes up or the first person who messages them on Facebook. This can cause a lot of problems down the road when they hire additional people because then their frame of reference is a bit skewed by this potentially problematic person that they worked with previously. A little more research and a little more vetting in the process of who you hire can alleviate bigger problems down the road.

How do you help them overcome these misconceptions and fears?

Claire E. Jones: There is a wellness aspect of what I do so I use neuroscience for a lot of my systems and frameworks. I'm certified through the NeuroLeadership Institute and I show people the science behind investing in their wellness and self-care and how that can bring their better selves to their businesses. This helps them better prioritize their time, basically filling their cup so that they can pour more into their business.

How do you help them implement the systems for lasting effects?

Claire E. Jones: I help them narrow their focus on what will give them the highest reward for their efforts. A lot of small business owners feel like they need to be on all the social platforms and doing all the latest things with ads or other shiny objects. It's called the *Shiny Object Syndrome*, where they come up with a new idea every week. They're like, well this is what is going to save the business and then they spend time going after all these new ideas without really getting anywhere. This is what I mean by taking a scattershot approach. They're trying too many things that aren't giving them quality ROI. I often see small business owners not being very strategic about where they're focusing their efforts.

When it comes to marketing strategies, you have to be on the platforms and the publications that your ideal demographic and client are on. For example, there's a rule of thumb that if you are accessing people for your customer base who are over 30 years old, you want to be on Facebook. If you are accessing people under 30 years old, you want to be on Instagram. But if you are a business-to-business organization, you need to be on LinkedIn. Or if you're accessing elder care services and senior care services, then maybe you want to consider doing a snail mail campaign because those people aren't hanging out on social media. It's all about targeting your efforts in a way that gives you a higher quality ROI and then you spend less time on it but get better results.

What inspired you to get into this line of work?

Claire E. Jones: I've been working with arts organizations and small businesses for 15 years and helping entrepreneurs is very much aligned with my core value of self-expression. Over the years, my love of these passion-driven businesses has deepened. I got my taste of it in 2014 when I opened up my first business. I graduated during the recession with an art history degree, which didn't give me many job options at the time. I figured that if no one else was going to hire me for a growth-oriented position, I was going to hire myself. I had been working in retail and small businesses since high school. So I figured opening up a retail shop was right up my alley.

That was my crash course in running my own business. I had seen behind the scenes for other businesses, but running one yourself is another level. I say I got my MBA via Google because if I didn't know it, I looked it up and learned it. From there, I pivoted into more business advisory roles because I realized that my background in research from art history paired well with my obsession with systems, I make systems for everything in my day to day life. That was a unique skill set when it came to helping small businesses develop and scale so I pivoted into more business advisory roles after closing down the store and eventually opened up this business in 2018.

One of the big lessons learned was to develop your market before you launch. It's important to spend the time and effort to develop your audiences and make sure that you have a group of people that you're able to launch your product or service to when you are ready to launch. Many people launch before developing their market so it takes a lot longer to then develop their market and get things sold. It's important for business owners to ask themselves how they are strategically planning for the future in their business. A lot of people in those positions don't necessarily consider that to be important right now because they're too busy putting out fires on a day to day basis. They don't feel like they have the bandwidth or the motivation to plan for the long term. You need to know where you're going, even if it doesn't go exactly according to plan (because nothing goes 100% according to plan), and have a general idea of where you're building the business to and what to do in order to get to that point.

About Claire E. Jones

Claire is the CEO of Liminal Clarity, a business development agency that acts as your trusted guide as you navigate the spaces between wellness and business, creativity and structure, as well as the transitions between the various stages of your business.

WEBSITE
ClarificationsCoaching.com

How to Feel Empowered to Create a Life You Love

Lindsay is showing people that they have the power to transform any aspect of their life. She works with organizations on team building and with individuals on getting what she calls a "Ph.D. in themselves "so that they can find their true purpose, and then be in service to humanity. Many people at some point in their life will feel stuck in some way, and Lindsay has developed processes and tools that get them unstuck and past any obstacle. She does this through coaching, courses and live events. The result is her clients have more confidence and more capacity to fulfill their dreams than ever before. They feel like they are now equipped to make positive things happen in those circumstances that arise that before would trigger them and cause roadblocks. They feel empowered to create a new life that they love.

Conversation with Lindsay Andreotti

How do you assess the challenges and roadblocks that are keeping your clients from reaching their full potential?

Lindsay Andreotti: It depends on the individual. What's fun about this is that sometimes they come in thinking that their biggest challenge is physical health but then turns into them getting a holistic view of themselves so they can make changes in many aspects of their lives, not just one. They choose a pathway that feels good to them. One aspect of the pathway might be individual coaching. One aspect might be joining a campfire chat with me and one of my many colleagues. One aspect may be coming to a live event where they're with a hundred other people who are working on something that they want to shift in their lives. Another aspect might be coming on one of our cruises or retreats. We do transformation education all around the world. And that's something that some people are inspired to go do. We call this transformation on vacation—and it's the best way to get out of old patterns and form new ones.

We show people the hologram of themselves, and then give them curriculum or tools that will enhance any aspect they deem most relevant. We have many ways that help people realize their limiting beliefs and overcome obstacles that are holding them back. Our participants learn about health and healing and about their physical bodies. They learn about shifting their mindset and reprogramming fear. They learn about emotional management and energy and how to use this vehicle called the human body to serve their experience of life. And they often find new friends that are doing the same things and will learn right alongside them, offering each other support.

What stops people from getting help from a coach?

Lindsay Andreotti: The biggest obstacle for most people getting help or guidance from a professional is not knowing if they truly need it. "When the student is ready, the teacher appears" is our motto, and we have found that the best time for anyone to have a coach is when they aren't really looking. One of the primary reasons they avoid hiring a coach is because they aren't sure that they're ready to let go of the thing that is holding them back from having what they want in life, or they truly don't know what they want. I meet dreamers every day of the week, and I'm always surprised by what holds them back from stepping toward their dream.

I find that it comes at a certain time in their life when people are ready. Typically two things inspire them to get started. One is so much pain that they can't stand the old pattern anymore. They're thinking, "Ugh, I've had it. I don't know, I gotta make a change." Or, they are so inspired to make a difference and to commit to themselves that they are just running like the wind and they need someone to support them on that trail. Every person is different, but those are the two thought patterns that generally get them to commit to change and find Earth.University.

Our participants are required to look at themselves as the creator of their experience and their life as their classroom. I have a process for reprogramming fear. I have a process for finding what lights them up. I have a process that shows them a roadmap of a strategy that will move them in the direction of their dreams. I have a bazillion tools, (I'll call it my toolkit) that comes out when I can pinpoint where the person is. So it's never a one size fits all. Come do this and you'll be transformed is the myth that is out there. No one thing will be a silver bullet to a better life, but that's the misconception that a lot of people are being told. We believe that every aspect of your life has a curriculum and we support our members in finding the right next learning opportunity for their growth and fulfillment.

When people hear about Earth.University for the first time, 99 out of a hundred people say, "Whoa, so cool. I want to know more about that." What happens in that early thought process is they begin to think about looking inward to find the answer that they've been looking for. It's difficult to determine what makes people finally decide to take the proactive steps necessary to lead a more fulfilling life. It's sort of like the caterpillar becoming a butterfly. A caterpillar does not know exactly why he/she is called to go on a certain day to build a cocoon, but they know that it's the right time and then they find the space to build the cocoon. Earth.University is a lot like the cocoon. It's a safe place to go to liquify what you've been and then become the fullest expression of what you're intended to be—the butterfly. That's why I call this process getting a Ph.D. in yourself because when people go through that process and they come out feeling like a whole new being that now has a new passion, purpose, and pattern. And the best part is, now they get to go hang with a bunch of other butterflies. Our alumni are some of the butterflies who have gone through the process.

Can you share an example?

Lindsay Andreotti: One of my colleagues was going through a transition in her career and she had been doing the same job for almost 15 years with the same company. She was finding herself feeling agitated, needing to do more, wanting something to change but didn't know exactly how to do it. At the same time, she was completely terrified to make a shift because of the common fears that we all experience. The money was good. She knew the job. She had a great relationship with the company and her boss. All the things that give us reason to go, "Ooh, I don't want to change that. I like what I've got." But at the same time, she was ready for a change and knew she needed to do something else, so we worked on a process with her that first revealed what lit her up and what it was about the change or the new version of herself that was really in alignment with where she needed to go? We then looked at a process for how to overcome the fear, how to reprogram the false fear that she had created and then developed a new story in her mind about how her current situation was going to be if she made a shift towards what she loved. We then created a roadmap of what that looked like and the five or six steps that she could take with her lights on to move toward her new vision.

The end result was creating a contract with her present employer that allowed her to go and do her dream while also continuing to work with the people she loved. It was a profound change in her life because she thought it had to be one or the other and she made up a huge story about how her present employer was going to make it hard for her to make this change. This ended up being mostly in her mind and she learned how to reprogram her patterns so she could have everything she wanted.

What is your inspiration?

Lindsay Andreotti: My own journey led me to how I help people today. Earth.University as a business, is a creation of what I wanted when I was about 30 years old. I had to overcome obstacles in my life. I had to face my fears. I had to learn what it takes to maximize this physical body of mine to be in service to my calling. I had to work on myself, my relationship with others, my career, my personality—everything. I felt the call as a caterpillar when I was 29, and I am still becoming my better and better butterfly self.

My inspiration was and continues to be pursuing my own Ph.D. in myself. Because of the curriculum I followed, and the ability to see what was happening while I was in the soup, I have now created a process for others to get their own Personal Hyper Drive (PHD) to their most satisfying life.

After 54 years on the planet, I finally feel like I've really gotten in touch with the magic of the human experience. I often say to entrepreneurs, if you're going to build a company around something that matters to you, scratch your own itch, something that truly matters to you and your personal experience of life will probably matter to a lot of other people.

That's what inspired me to create Earth.University. I began to recognize that my soul came to this earth in a human form so that I could learn and grow and that everything about my life has been my classroom. I simply turned it back around to look at and find gratitude for the entire experience that was me.

It is a very powerful and rewarding process to show others how to do the same thing in their lives. What inspires me is lighting people up and helping them get on with their dreams. Our passions and dreams are pre-programmed, and we learn by continuing to learn, grow, and understand that we are the creators of our experiences. I also really enjoy connecting people to other people (butterfly to butterfly) that are working on similar stuff so that more dreams can be fulfilled and more leading-edge thought can come into a new evolved reality.

Three core lessons have profoundly shifted me into what became the core of Earth.University. Number one, I learned about the conditioned mind and how it does not need to define who I am. Number two, I learned what it takes to reprogram fear so that in any moment when I feel triggered, scared or otherwise, I know how to check in with myself and quickly evaluate whether I'm safe or unsafe, is it real or imagined and what I can control about it. I know how to reprogram negative thoughts quickly. That one tool has been a huge lesson for how to navigate life with a lot more ease and grace. The third thing is about how to see life in its fullness is just one thing being expressed in infinite numbers of ways. The dark, the light, the good, the bad, as perfect just as it is. Life is a learning environment. So rich and so powerful, you can't get it in any other experience. That's what makes it fun to be human.

I encourage people to ask themselves questions if they are considering working with a coach. Questions like: What do I not know about myself that is getting in the way? Why is this pattern continuing to happen? What is that? Why is it that I always choose the wrong person for my love relationship? Why is it that my boss in every job I've ever had always seems to turn out to be this kind of person? Why it's annoying and it keeps showing up. Ask the WHY question, why did this happen?

The second kind of question is, what's my purpose in life? I know it's more than what I'm doing right now, but I don't know what it is. Third question, how can I be the very best version of me and what would that be like if I was? With these questions and a few new tools, perspectives, and support, we all have the ability to become powerful creators and contributors to humanity. Welcome to Earth.University!

About Lindsay Andreotti

Chief Experience Officer, Earth. University and Brilliance Enterprises. With over 30 years of Sales, HR and Organizational Development experience, Lindsay has assisted in the start, growth, and development of over 100 companies, small and large, in public, private, and non-profit arenas.

WEBSITE
Earth.University

How To Improve Communication Strategies for Personal and Business Growth

Productive businesses require effective relationships. Even more importantly, they require effective relationships between the leadership and their direct reports. Over 20 years working 1:1 and with groups has made this clear to Denise Miller, head of Leadership Ninja Coaching. She coaches organizations and entrepreneurs on how to improve their ability to authentically support, understand, lead, network, direct, connect, and communicate. She helps people have better relationships through understanding the formation of the mind and by becoming aware of inauthentic, disempowered thoughts and behaviors. People release the fears and misconceptions holding them back so they are free to have better relationships in all parts of their lives.

Conversation with Denise Miller

How do you help people communicate better?

Denise Miller: I help people open their minds to what is between themselves and having better relationships. We hear a lot these days about the importance of increasing emotional intelligence to keep us from offending others around us. Most of us would naturally have had this sensitivity – what happened?

I believe it comes down, in part, to the way we are raised. From the time we're young, we have people around us that have their own opinions, beliefs, fears, and preferences. They implant and impress those onto us because they think it's our best chance to be safe and succeed. Maybe it was truly required for the world they grew up in. It's not necessarily true for the current or next generations. As a result, we grow with a nebulous, somewhat unrealistic idea about how we can best get along in the world, the people we should like or fear, and the people we should control, AKA bully, or bend over backward to gain the approval of.

The side of this that many don't think about is those who bear the weight of believing constant improvement is required to be safe and successful. Never feeling enough, always striving to be better. Some people believe that every sacrifice is worthwhile to become financially stable (AKA safe) and pass that 'work ethic' on to their children. There is a difference between a good work ethic and perfectionism; never feeling good enough. The instilled or embedded need for constant improvement to feel acceptable is a heavy load to bear – for children as well as adults. This way of being will often lead to people judging themselves, life, and others as never measuring up. It shows up as chronic stress and anxiety. You may hear internal reminders to 'be a good girl/boy' if you listen closely to your inner voice. As a result, some people grow up without the ability to simply be who they are, assess the other person in the moment, and be in an appropriate relationship with them.

We all want to be accepted and understood. That's why we want to connect and communicate in the first place. Many people go around with the appearance of emotional intelligence. They've been taught what emotional intelligence should sound and look like. They have read an article something like; *"If You Use these 12 Terms, You Are Not Emotionally Intelligent,"* encouraging people to have the appearance of sensitivity instead of finding out how they became desensitized in the first place. I help people get to the basis of how they relate and then improve from there.

Can you share an example of how you helped a client overcome their limitations?

Denise Miller: I worked with a client recently who was a serial job quitter. She was never satisfied and she just kept saying, "This isn't the job for me." She came to me looking for authenticity, which is hugely important. However, we don't have much of an idea about what authenticity truly is because at first, it is simply coming from those false opinions, beliefs, fears, and preferences of those that raised us. We think that's authenticity.

This client discovered that a point arrives for her where she knows she has to move on. She could identify it quite clearly. It was when suddenly her boss was no longer providing her the safety, security, and feelings of success that she needed to have from a job. And so she would move on. She realized that if the person she worked for was transferred or left the organization she would usually need to leave. We began working to develop ways she can support herself so she doesn't need those indicators of success and safety to come from the current leader. Those can come from herself. That is authenticity. So far, we're doing well with this. So far, she hasn't left the job. She thought she had to. She is now noticing that she was pinning a parental role onto her bosses and that's not what she needs in her life anymore.

How do you identify the obstacles that are holding people back?

Denise Miller: I look at the relational obstacles people face in three different categories – I call it Relationship Diagnostics. First, we identify what is going on between me and this other person that I'd want to have a better relationship with. It could be that I want to be their leader. It could be that they're my boss. It could be a personal relationship, a family member. If the relationship isn't going well or if there are obstacles in the relationship, then generally they are in three areas. I use the acronym C.A.R. I consider C.A.R. a vehicle to a better relationship.

C stands for communication. How is the communication between yourself and this other person? Do you feel free to be able to speak directly? Are you communicating at appropriate times? If you think your communication style is just fine and it's still coming from the past, loaded with those opinions, beliefs, fears, stresses, and preferences, then your communication is coming through loaded with those preconceived notions. We can all open to more direct communication and it might be clunky at first because it's coming from a different place. However, if it wasn't an issue, they probably wouldn't be having this problem.

I believe that everyone has the potential to develop and have healthy relationships with others. I also believe having positive relations with others is one of the reasons we are on this planet. So, if it's not natural, then I help people find out why it's not natural for them. What experience, for example, is causing this break in connection. Just knowing that others think I don't have emotional intelligence or sensitivity isn't going to open me up to have it. In sessions, we work together to find out what happened, why we developed a communication that isn't working.

A is affinity. Affinity is likeability. Due to societal implants or impressions, we decide from a young age that there are certain people we like and certain people we don't like, and we go with it. We might try to put on a persona of emotional intelligence by telling ourselves; 'Even though that person triggers me, I'm acting as if I like them because I'm emotionally intelligent now.' What's happened is that the person doesn't realize they can originate affinity. I can just decide to like somebody, I can decide to like someone completely different than me. I can decide to like someone, even if they remind me of someone that was abusive and traumatized me in my past. I could still decide to like someone in completely different ways than I have – I don't have to agree with people to simply be ok with them. Now we're going a little deeper than simple emotional intelligence.

R is the final piece of C.A.R. It stands for reality. If we live in a glass box and we're not aware of the reality of the people around us, then we're unable to deeply understand them or be in a relationship with them. We might have somebody that shows up constantly late for work and we just may keep on telling them, you have to show up, you have to show up. At the same time, we don't even understand the reality of their daily commute, or their family, or their trauma – and until we do, we can't really be in reality with their situation and we can't truly be in a leadership relationship with them either.

What are the most common obstacles your clients come to you for help with?

Denise Miller: People write articles and papers inventing buzz-words and phrases that give us the idea there's something wrong with us and we should fix it. There's one that's being used quite a bit these days called the *Imposter Syndrome.*

Many people think things like, "I am not good enough, here I am doing this work, but I'm an imposter. I'm not an expert. Here I am trying to be an expert. Everyone says that you need to be the expert and so I'm trying to be the expert, but I'm going to get caught. I'm going to be seen and exposed as not the expert." This is not a syndrome. It's a fact of human nature. It's quite interesting as you work long term with clients as I have over the years. I'll have a young entrepreneur that wants to build their business authentically come to me and we'll start exploring their vision, their mission, what it's going to look like and sound like. We work on the deeper levels of branding. We're coming in on a solid foundation. It's just wonderful how inspiring these young people are because they don't know much but they have confidence. They tell themselves, "I'm going to do this, I'm going to solve this problem." Young entrepreneurs come in free of a lot of the inhibitions that develop as we get older.

With more experience, people start realizing how little they actually know compared to all there is to know – and begin to have self-limiting thoughts like: "I don't have the right to be here," "That person said this much better than I did," "Who am I to think I know this?" It's a natural part of human transitional growth. People start out thinking that we can conquer the world, then reality hits and our fears and doubts, our opinions and impressions and preferences of others, start knocking us back. We are simply facing reality and need to develop trust in our path, our value, and our authenticity.

I am working with a client now and she's one of these young excited people. She is getting a natural following on social media generated by her enthusiasm. People are coming to her and asking, "How can I learn from you?" She also sees comments that she seems angry. She feels it is her passion. We began working on how she is expressing herself and she identified that anytime she feels confronted, or if somebody is pushing against the belief systems she has developed, that she feels 'a monster' arises inside her. She now knows that the monster tries to take control through dominance and anger whenever she is confronted and feels victimized. We each have our roadblocks and they're built into how we decided success and safety looked like when we were young. We can clear these hidden personas.

What inspired you to get into this type of work?

Denise Miller: I started as a professional speaker, speaking to youth and adults telling stories that would inspire them. Once I was invited to come and speak at a place where women were getting breast cancer checkups to talk about facing fears and supporting each other. I wrote an article about the healing power of that kind of storytelling and then a local university asked me if I would speak to their graduating health practitioner classes about listening with their whole self. They had identified an ongoing problem due to students making assumptions and not getting the authentic ability to diagnose through receiving all available information the person is communicating – including non-verbal.

I taught that class for the next 15 years. During that time, I trained extensively to become better at teaching people how to 'listen with their whole self'. I now utilize these skills in 1:1 coaching as well as group training. I still love speaking, I still love helping people see each other more clearly. The piece that has the biggest impact on me is when people realize the problems, they're coming to me to solve are really in their mind and if they had clearer thinking they could have easily handled the problem on their own.

I especially love it when a client takes charge of limiting beliefs. They are often amazed at the new opportunities they see. Opportunities that they never thought possible before are suddenly options because they no longer believe they are less than up to the challenge.

About Denise Miller

Denise Miller is a relational communication, leadership, and mindset expert. She has a unique ability to entertain, engage and educate while presenting exciting new information on the connections of the body, mind, heart and soul. Denise combines her love of story, and her fascination with people to offer an eye-opening new look at face reading, body language, communication dynamics and the intricacies of the mind.

WEBSITE
DeniseMiller.ca

A Leading Voice for Millennials With Tourette's

Paula Jean Ferri is an author, an advocate, and a motivational speaker who helps millennials with Tourette syndrome to see their individual strengths and use them to their advantage.

Ferri works with millennials who have a tendency to apologize too often and feel like they're struggling to catch a break in their lives.

She encourages millennials with tics to develop goals by positively using their energy rather than fighting against themselves. In addition, she helps them see their weaknesses as strengths and show them how to utilize it.

Conversation with Paula Jean Ferri

What are some common struggles for millennials with Tourette Syndrome?

Paula Jean Ferri: I've seen millennials with Tourette Syndrome struggle a lot with self-confidence, feeling like they don't have any kind of control over their lives. Some have the mentality that they can't catch a break or even date someone.

Finding a job is another area; not feeling like they have or can achieve their purpose. Sometimes tics can be so severe that they can't hold traditional jobs.

Lack of control their lives and being unable to have a traditional job prevent them from seeing how they're able to fully contribute because they're lacking in these very key areas.

How is working with you different for others with Tourette's Syndrome?

Paula Jean Ferri: I believe what's different and unique about me is I do not try to change who you are and the traits that you have. My goal is to help you use all of your traits to your advantage rather than fighting against yourself.

I have Tourette's as well. I actually did not start ticking until I was 17 years old. I thought it was just like a continual hiccup that didn't hurt. Days went by, and then weeks, and then months. Seven years later, when I was 24, I was officially diagnosed with Tourette Syndrome. But over those years, they went from just a normal hiccup to various types of animal noises and I developed a shoulder tic.

I think being diagnosed so much later in life actually gave me more of an advantage rather than a disappointment or discouragement. It was more of "Finally, there's a name for what I've been doing," and I also was much more in control of my treatment. Understanding that this was not something I could control, as a child, I was told that it develops later in life, and this helped me gain that unique perspective that allows me to teach others the same principles.

Who do you help?

Paula Jean Ferri: I coach individuals with tics. People were always telling me that I should help others because I had such a great attitude about my diagnosis. I haven't let it hold me back or hinder me; it's funny because, for many years, I just thought it was hiccups. I was still a fully functioning, capable human being. Hearing so often from people and seeing the contrast between my life and others, I'm not special in any way. I have Tourette's, just like other millennials, and I want them to experience the same fullness of purpose, joy, and fulfillment that can come when you're not held back by the Tourette syndrome.

All people have issues. That's just a fact. The difference is that there are people who understand how to use those issues as a benefit, no matter if it's Tourette syndrome or any other kind of disability. These things are difficult, but they also give us an opportunity to become better and stronger. They actually give us a fair advantage if we know how to utilize them. As millennials, we're old enough to take control of our own treatments. Some of us may have been diagnosed as a child and our parents and doctors told us what to do and how to treat it, but now, we can take control of our own treatments. We can take control of our own lives and our ability to contribute to the world around us.

How do you help others look at the diagnosis differently and use challenges as strengths?

Paula Jean Ferri: The biggest advantage of having tics that I found is the allocation of resources. I'm able to use my energy to hold down tics for hours on end. Now, I can focus that energy toward something productive. I can use that energy to write a book. I can use that energy to a conversation with someone. I can use that energy in my relationships without ending up so exhausted. Instead of fighting against ourselves, we can work on something much more purposeful, worthwhile, and enjoyable. Let's make it happen.

What are some myths and misconceptions about Tourette Syndrome?

Paula Jean Ferri: Most of what I see in the Tourette Syndrome support groups and within the transgender community is that everyone is so focused on what medication works and makes it go away. However, even with medication, tics are usually only placated and never actually disappear. So, the biggest myth is that the only way to be normal and happy is to have a life without tics, whether it be through medication or other holistic routines to help reduce the tics and make us more functional. Yes, there are a few lucky ones that may see their tics disappear, but for those who continue to tic, there is a way to utilize and work with them rather than against them.

What are some challenges to having Tourette Syndrome?

Paula Jean Ferri: Many individuals with Tourette's are still living at home because they feel like their ticks get in the way of a normal functional life.

I have seen supportive mentors in the community. One thing that I love about people with Tourette's is how compassionate they are. The second they hear about someone with Tourette's, they will drop everything to talk with them and make sure that they're okay and give them space to talk and to get to know one another.

I'm not saying that I can or cannot make tics disappear. I'm not a medical professional. However, I can help you make a significant change within your life because seeing this diagnosis as a strength has been a complete game-changer for me, and knowing how to utilize it gives you so much more purpose and direction.

What are some common fears for those with Tourette's?

Paula Jean Ferri: Individuals living with Tourette's experience many fears so anxiety is a highly connected Comorbid. There are too many fears to list. Dealing with Tourette's can be difficult. People don't feel they are in control of their body. It's easy to be afraid of how others are going to respond. There are kids who are picked on or beaten because of things that they say or do. Constant movement can be exhausting, much less going outside of that sphere and into the society and looking at those prejudices and misconceptions.

How can individuals get past those challenges and fears?

Paula Jean Ferri: Rather than focusing on all the things that we can't control, let's focus on how much control we do have and what we can do. We don't have to listen to anyone except ourselves. We (those with Tourette's) know our bodies the best. We are the ones that can determine that treatment and taking control one step at a time allows that control, ability, and confidence to really expand.

What are some misconceptions about Tourette Syndrome?

Paula Jean Ferri: Tourette syndrome often starts in childhood. There are some deep-rooted beliefs about what to do and how to take care of it, especially from parents and doctors. The diagnosis often starts out as misdirected because it's so easy to miss. Kids can go undiagnosed for years, and they're often told things like, "Stop misbehaving!" We're not bad kids. We're not broken in any way. We don't need fixing; we're human beings and have thoughts, opinions, hopes, dreams, and a right to pursue just like any other human being. Some kids don't grow up understanding their own voice and power and continuing with that mindset into adulthood can really hold us back.

What are some common mistakes made by someone with Tourette Syndrome?

Paula Jean Ferri: One very common mistake is, again, seeing Tourette's as a weakness rather than strength and utilizing it properly. Another pitfall is, getting stuck in our own heads. Again, being indoctrinated from such a young age, we tend to think that this is the way it has to be. Tourette's is not a joke; however, we can use that energy toward something much more productive.

How can you help those with Tourette Syndrome?

Paula Jean Ferri: I can help them see what a huge difference a small change in the state of mind can have in the long-term. Tics vary from person to person. Everyone has a completely different experience, and making even just that small shift in that small area can be a huge eye-opening, life-changing experience, much less other multiple mind-shift changes that can happen.

I want people with a tics diagnosis to understand that some of the challenges they're having are also common challenges that people that don't have Tourette's have. At a surface level, it may be very different. We have different experiences, but yes, deep down at the core, we all essentially have the same issues, same worries and concerns.

Do you have a success story you can share?

Paula Jean Ferri: A woman in one of the support groups was seeking advice about her teenage daughter. This poor girl also had cop, and unfortunately, she was often picked on, bullied, beaten by her peers for saying things that she had no control over.

I sent this girl a copy of my first book, *Awkwardly Strong*, and we've had a few conversations after she received my book, and she's been very grateful to see and understand that she's not alone.

She needed to understand how much more control she has of the people that she allows into her life. She didn't necessarily have to spend time around the people that are constantly bullying her. If she's not around them, they don't hear the phrases, and she can be around people who lift and encourage her and may find it more fun or who don't pay attention to what she's saying. She needed to have control over the type of people that she allowed into her life, especially on a constant basis. Realizing this was a huge relief for her. That one little shift makes a huge difference in our lifestyle patterns.

Who is your ideal client?

Paula Jean Ferri: I'm looking to work one-on-one with someone who's wanting to make a change in their life. I enjoy working with millennials; they tend to have a lot going on in their lives that they want to try and pursue, but I can work with any particular age. I can also help parents to realize the benefits of this.

What lessons have you learned?

Paula Jean Ferri: When I was in college, before I was diagnosed, I still believed that these were hiccups. I was taking a class on narrative identity and culture, which basically talks about how everything that we experience around us is some form of a story. Just like fiction and nonfiction stories, and we choose which ones to believe. I soon realized that the culture around me and the things that people around me were saying weren't necessarily gospel truths. I also recognized my ability to control those stories and my own life. Now I can create the future that I want. I can create the culture around me, and I can influence others around me. Whatever we've made up, we can also change.

What questions should someone with Tourette Syndrome be asking?

Paula Jean Ferri: "How much is this really benefiting me?" We should recognize what's most important and ultimately what's going to get us where we want to be.

I'm not saying that parents and doctors are trying to ruin our lives, but we must understand that they might be misguided or misdirected. We need to ask ourselves, "How is this benefiting me?" And if it's not benefitting you, let it go. Also ask yourself, "How is this medication/relationship benefiting me?"

If the relationship is not beneficial, they don't have to stay in your life. You have that choice. It's all about your mindset. The books that you read, the shows that you watch; how is it benefiting you? How is it helping you to become what you want to become?

How can fear be used as a benefit?

Paula Jean Ferri: As I mentioned before, having Tourette Syndrome can cause so much fear and anxiety, and that can be debilitating. When we recognize that fear can be used as an asset, and we realize how to utilize that and some other different things, we can help reduce anxiety attacks or panic attacks.

I've included in my book some tips to come out of panic attacks and anxiety attacks because the level of fear that we're experiencing is too extreme. But at the same time, fear can also be beneficial; it can be utilized as a strength. That's a common theme throughout all of my books. We're awkwardly strong, tragically strong, and fearfully strong. Fear isn't something that should be holding us back. It actually is an advantage that we need to learn how to utilize.

Do you have any final comments?

Paula Jean Ferri: Know that you're not alone; you're not the first to have Tourette syndrome. You're not the last either. You're not the first to face hard times, and you won't be the last. But this is your individual life. You have your own unique story to create, and you're the one that gets to determine the ending. And then, from there, all you have to do is figure out how to get there, which I would love to help with because I want to see you get there. I want to see you have your story as you see it and to have the life that you want.

How can someone find out more about you and your books?

Paula Jean Ferri: My book *Fearfully Strong* is available on Amazon. I also have a blog on www.medium.com. My social media handle is @Jesssquaks, which is also my handle on Facebook, Instagram, and Twitter.

I am also working on creating a soothe kit that will go hand-in-hand with the *Fearfully Strong* message. I recommend a soothe kit because if we can get outside of our own heads, with one of our five senses, it can usually help bring us out of panic attacks. Everything included in the kit will help with the panic attacks, and each item in the kit is something that you can see, hear, taste, touch, and smell. The kits are small enough to fit in a purse or a backpack.

About Paula Jean Ferri

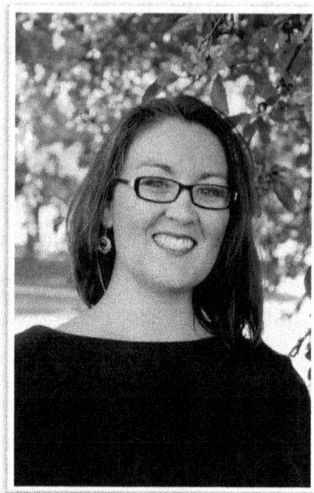

Paula Jean Ferri is one of the most awkward people you will ever meet. She often screams and makes animal noises in public, sometimes even during work meetings and church services. Having been in multiple awkward situations, she has become a master at the weird and uncomfortable. While always an oddball, the uncontrollable noises started her senior year of high school. At age 24, she was diagnosed with Tourette Syndrome.

Growing up in a small town called Logandale, it wasn't always easy to stick out so much. So, upon graduating from high school, she went from small town to small town, attending college in Ephraim, Utah, to attend Snow College before transferring to Laie, Hawaii, to finish her undergrad in International Cultural Studies with an emphasis in Communications at Brigham Young University, Hawaii.

She currently resides in Salt Lake City, Utah, where she not only writes but sings, dances, hikes, watches old movies, and dreams of the day she can go back to Hawaii and travel the world. Paula Jean is actively involved with her church, attending not only Sunday meetings but also serving in the temple, leading the choir in her congregation, and playing sports with the youth. She also loves her visits home to hang out with her family and the three coolest nephews in the world.

EMAIL
jesssqueaks@gmail.com

FACEBOOK
Facebook.com/JessSqueaks

TWITTER
@jesssqueaks

INSTAGRAM
@jesssqueaks

Thinking Big with The National Association of Local Businesses

Joe Grushkin is the CEO and Founder of the National Association of Local Businesses. His company offers over 100 top quality products and services for local businesses, at discounted pricing normally reserved for much larger companies. Membership is free! In this interview, Joe shares his journey of how he went from a young, ambitious college student on a summer job, to be instrumental in the company's international expansion and ultimately inducted into the Vector/Cutco "Hall of Fame" and becoming a "serial entrepreneur" for over 35 years and is now the CEO of the National Association of Local Businesses.

To learn more about Joe Grushkin and the National Association of Local Businesses, go to: http://www.NAOLB.com.

Conversation with Joe Grushkin

Give us a little background on yourself and what you are working on. How did you come up with what you're doing right now?

Joe Grushkin: I started my career when I was going into my senior year of college and I sold Cutco knives as a summer job. I was there in the beginning when they had only 11 sales offices and when I got started, I was the top rep in New England and number three in the nation. I earned about ten thousand dollars at my summer job, which would be the equivalent of about $40,000 or $50,000 today. I really enjoyed it, and I got tagged to go to the Manager Training Program in my senior year. When I graduated, I became a Sales Manager for Cutco in Stanford, Connecticut.

During my previous summer with Cutco, there was a record-breaking year by a Summer Manager who did a $183,000 in business. He was the top guy in the company with that performance. I said I was going to beat that, and everybody thought I was just a cocky kid coming in. That year, we did over $210,000 in sales for the summer, and I earned about $40,000. In today's dollars, I would have earned about $120,000 that first summer. So, it was a pretty good run. I did it through productivity, by training salespeople. The average sales rep back then did about $800 in sales. My first summer, my salespeople did $2,000 per person. That would be $8,000 per rep in today's dollars.

Two years later, I moved to Boston. I went to New England as a Division Manager and started my own office. Three years later, we had 18 sales offices throughout New England. Then they asked me to go to Canada as the National Sales Manager of Canada. I started out with five transplanted managers. Seven years later, we had fifty-five offices and 5500 salespeople. We trained over 20,000 salespeople in my career, and I was inducted into the Cutco "Hall of Fame" in 1991. I retired in 1997 at the age of 37—it was it was a fun ride.

Were you inherently a good salesperson? How did you know what to do?

Joe Grushkin: I needed a summer job; I was bartending for the summer and in between semesters and I just needed something to do during the day. My mom would yell at me even though I made good money bartending. She'd say, "Go get a job!" A friend of mine started working with Cutco so I went to the training and next thing you know, I was helping the Manager run the office. I really got the bug.

Was I a good salesperson? I don't know, it was a great program, it was a great training ground, and there's a systemic process. When I became a Manager myself, I saw areas to make it better and I applied that to what I thought would be beneficial to people who were in my shoes just a year earlier. So, I saw ways to make it better and that's why the productivity skyrocketed the way it did.

You had a process or a system to follow from Cutco, but then you just put your own spin on it and made it better. Isn't that just the lifeblood of entrepreneurism?

Joe Grushkin: The first summer, I did it the way they told me to do it. I just did it with my own personality and style. There's an old story about salespeople. The story goes that there was an insurance company that had a sales guy who was the best sales guy three years running. They had hundreds and hundreds of salespeople, but this guy did three times more business than everybody else, every year, year in and year out. So, they brought in a consulting company to study this guy, and they watched what he ate, what he drank, how much he slept, and what his family was like. They checked his background all the way to Kindergarten to talk to his teachers. They did a deep dive on him and they put together this huge analysis. It cost millions of dollars, as the story goes. They did this analysis and discovered he just did what they told them, three times more often.

When you look at what people do to be successful, the person who's going to go out and work harder and focus on the basics and focus on the skillset that they laid out as a success formula is going to do the best. Anybody can be successful, but it's the "can do" mindset that gets you there. It's the mindset of doubt, apprehension, lethargy and distractions that causes failure. The idea here is that I just went out and blindly did what they told me to do. They said, "Call people this many times a day," I did. They said, "Go out and see people and prospect" and, "Read the script this way, and put your personality into it" and that's what made me successful with that career.

What lead you to start the National Association of Local Businesses?

In 2007, I noticed flat screen TVs were getting bigger and cheaper. I also knew that most advertising, radio, TV advertising, newspapers and magazines were dying and very difficult to work with, and very expensive with low results, especially for small businesses. One thing my clients kept asking me, "How do I get more local business?" So, I noticed the trend of the TV's getting bigger and cheaper and I said, "I wonder if we can put advertising on the TV at a low price so local businesses can get exposure?" This was before Times Square had digital walls everywhere, before out of home marketing was really prevalent. We hung up a TV in the local deli of my town and between Thanksgiving and New Year's I sold 30 ads to go on that screen. (If anybody ever says you can't sell between Thanksgiving and New Year's, please have them contact me, I'll talk to them for you!) I knew that we had a great concept.

Fast forward, three years later we had 350 screens around the country, a network of independent salespeople selling ads on screens, and we were doing over $2 million in sales in our third year. It was really going gangbusters until I noticed two things happened. One, I was sitting in the deli looking up at the screen. I looked down and there was a line of people, but they weren't looking at the screen. They were all looking at this black device in their palm of their hand. It's 2010 and this interesting thing came out; it was called the smart phone! Everybody had one all of the sudden and I knew that it took the eyeballs off the screens and onto the palm of their hand. The other thing that I noticed was our customers—and we had thousands of them across the country—started calling us up saying, "Love the screens, but what's a tweet?" And, "How do I use Facebook?" We really didn't have an answer for them at the time. So, I got together with my daughter and her boyfriend (now her husband.) I said to them, "I think this Face-thing is going to be big!" They still give me a hard time for calling it a "face-thing," because I didn't really know what was.

Nobody in small business understood, in 2010, what this "social media" thing was. Nobody understood the "Internet" thing. They just knew that it was out there, and they didn't know how to deal with it. I said to the kids (Aly Grushkin Carter and son-in-law, Alex Carter) and said, "Let's figure out how to do this." After that, we started to expand our network of customers to manage social media. As matter of fact, in 2011, the words "Social Media Manager" were not even in Wikipedia, it didn't exist.

We started managing social media for small businesses by posting content to Facebook and monitoring and responding to reviews on Yelp. Facebook and Google didn't even have review sections at that time. At the time, we would build the Google page so they could get found and this was revolutionary. For a few hundred bucks a month, our customers expanded nationwide, again through a network of independent salespeople. Over the next six years we expanded our product line because Instagram, Pinterest, YouTube and LinkedIn all came out with social sites, and review sites came out too. We managed all those platforms for our customers in addition to listing services and website design, SEO and Email Marketing and advertising through Google, Facebook, Twitter and LinkedIn. In other words, we became a full-service agency over the next six years, with over 80 different products and services available, specifically for small businesses, at really discounted pricing.

Again, I noticed the trends changing (as an entrepreneur you've got to keep your head on a swivel and notice what's going on around you! You can't have blinders on.) I noticed that in 2018, if I walked into a business with a salesperson and talked about social media they'd say. "You're the fifth person in here today." Or, I'd go to a networking event and there were 5 people who stood up and said, "I do social media. I do websites. I do this. I do that." I said, these people were in high school when I got started! I realized we needed to differentiate ourselves as a company.

I started to connect with businesses that provided services to small business and local business owners. Then, I realized that local businesses and independent businesses weren't getting the kind of deep discounts bigger companies routinely got offered. They weren't getting volume benefits and they weren't getting serviced like the big companies were. So, we cobbled together 45 products and services from different vendors and put them all under one umbrella called the National Association of Local Businesses.

Today, the National Association of Local Businesses provides over 100 products and services at discounted pricing, normally reserved for much larger companies. With our collective buying power, we bring together top-quality products and services so that local independent businesses can be more profitable, productive, and promoted to more customers. Membership in the association is totally free. So, all our members do is pay for the services they use and when they do, they're getting better pricing than they can get if they weren't part of the membership.

We've expanded this across the country through what we call an Ambassador Network. Our Ambassadors get access to these products and services so they can sell them to local businesses. Or, if they are already selling to local businesses, now they can bring in 100 additional products. They become the "go to" person in that community for everything marketing related. It's almost like that businessperson who comes in and the National Association of Local Businesses comes in like a partner, so that Ambassador can almost become their own agency and the agency offers all of those things because they now have the people in place to fulfill all the different local business's needs, without having to fulfill their needs themselves.

For instance, they can offer, not only the social media products and services that we have under the MaxExposure brand, but accounting services, or even funding. Let's say somebody wants to do a $10,000 advertising campaign, we have a partner that will provide them a credit line to be able to get that cash to be able to do that advertising. We have credit card processing with an average of 2.3% per transaction or in some cases through some really cool programs to get pricing down to as low as zero for the merchant. We have printing, and an automobile concierge service, so somebody can get a car for their daughter who's going to college, or a fleet for their sales team.

We have a LinkedIn consultant and software that will help a business prospect on LinkedIn through automation. Could you imagine sending out 100 individual messages a day to connect with people in a specific market or group, so that you can target them, connect with them, and then engage with them through messenger, rather than just advertising? That software cost less than $100 a month. We have over 100 products and services.

Is there one or two really unique products within the National Association of Local Businesses?

One of the coolest things we have is a tele-medicine program. Could you imagine the mom who has three kids, it's 3 in the morning—that's the only time of the day that your 4-year-old gets the ear infection. So, you have three kids, dad is traveling, it's the middle of the winter, it's cold and nasty out, and your kid is screaming with an ear infection. So, you've got to get them all in snowsuits, load them all into the car, take them to the ER, or urgent care and deal with that. Could you imagine instead of that, logging on, having a video chat with a board-certified doctor, in this country, having that conversation, they diagnose it, they call or send the prescription to your local CVS or Walgreens and you can pick up that prescription right in your neighborhood, and have that kid taken care of without having to take them all to the doctor and sit in a waiting room?

We offer that program to businesses, so they can offer it to their employees. Now, the real benefit is that a local pizza place that has four waitresses and two cooks, he can't afford an $800 dollar a month insurance package to keep his employees as part of this company. But, could you imagine if he offered them tele-medicine for $25 a month, he pays or maybe he splits it with them, whatever he wants to do. It's $25 a month and unlimited use and covers the employee's entire family?

Most people don't even know services like that exist! We have traditional medical insurance that will cut your rates in half and it's in 42 states. We have IT support. We even have a guy who delivers hot tubs anywhere in the country. Our range of products and services is really very diverse, and we've built it with the mindset that it's time small business owners get some benefit—that they're not just a random independent businesses, that we should consolidate them all together, and bring them services so they, in turn, have the opportunity to not only save money, but level the playing field with the big guys.

Our Ambassador Network is the real magic to this. So, our ambassadors are of that face of the business in that community and our Ambassador Network is beautiful because it pays commissions for the life of the customer. This is the closest thing a sales person can get to long term residual income, because as long as they are connected to that customer, and the customers buying products and services and using them on a monthly or recurring basis, the commissions are paid the Monday after the sale is created. That becomes a powerful income stream for an independent salesperson.

Ambassadors come in two flavors; there's the B2B salesperson, for instance, they're out selling advertising, or insurance, or consulting services, or they may be selling magazine ads, or radio ads, they are independent salespeople typically. Consultants are great resources for ambassadors because they're always talking to people, and they're always being asked, "How can I fix this?" When they refer the products and services under the National Association of Local Businesses umbrella, they get a piece of that action for the life of that customer. That commission can be 30% all the way up to 60%, depending on their level with the company. Those commissions continue for the life of the customer, and we have customers that go all the way back to 2011 when we started. So, they stick around for a long, long time.

So, if you're a business owner and you have employees, whether it's 1 or 100, you can become an Ambassador to the National Association of Local Businesses through you, and generate commissions on services that your employees use anyway?

Joe Grushkin: If you're a salesperson and you're selling to businesses, you can become an ambassador with the National Association of Local Businesses. Let's use an example with a business coach named Becky. Becky works with business owners. So, if Becky was an ambassador and those business owners said, "Becky, do you know anybody who does a website?" And she said, "Yeah, the National Association of Local Businesses, let me connect you and create an appointment for you with them." If that businessowner buys a website, Becky gets the commission on that. Her client, in this case, would get a better deal than if they went out and shopped 10 other companies.

Now the other side of that, is let's say there's a company that sells to businesses, they sell magazine advertising, and the magazine goes to the community and they sell advertising in the community. When they walk in the door to a business, it's either buy an ad, "yes"; buy an ad, "no," it's a binary sales process. If they walk in and they say they want to buy an ad, when they come back next month, what is there to sell them?

There's only another ad to sell them, or they buy a year's worth of advertising and then they never see that person again. Now, if they buy an ad, they can come back next month and say, "Hey, let's take a look at your credit card rates, or would you like to get a digital ad where everyone who receives the magazine in that town will also see an ad on Facebook for your business?" Now they can sell them a Facebook ad.

What if you don't have that type of business in your association?

Joe Grushkin: You name it, we have it. And if we don't, we have sources to find it. We're expanding. We take on only vetted service providers. Out of the 45 service providers we currently have, I've known 40 of them personally for over 20 years. In addition, they have to be capable of servicing a nationwide audience at this juncture. They also need to prove that they can give us better pricing, and they are contracted to make sure that our customers receive some kind of better pricing, or additional services, over and above what a normal price would give them. So, we've vetted them, we've contracted them, and they are committed to the long term of our association. The other side of the coin is, the ones I didn't know, were referred to me, we've purchased from them, we did our due diligence.

The next generation of the National Association of Local Businesses will work like this: When we have a footprint in a local area of enough ambassadors and enough engagement, we're going to look for high quality local providers. We'll have landscapers, painters, and roofers, and car detailing, local housecleaning, and local businesses like restaurants and hospitality. Local businesses will give our members an additional discount.

We've been working at it for a while and we continue to focus on the next generation. To be very frank, and I don't talk pie in the sky for anybody... this is a 6-figure income for an Ambassador. An Ambassador who makes just two sales a week can generate $80,000 to $100,000 in the first year. Because of the residual, they can see well upwards of $150,000-$200,000 in the second year. We've proven this out. It's a real opportunity. We are selling territories so that people can actually own the business in a county within our business. Those are the people who are going to get the 60% commission, the owners, and then they can hire full time salespeople to work for them. Follow the thinking here: You hire somebody for

$350, $400 a week, to be out there talking to businessowners, and pay them 10% of the commissions on what they generate. We pay 60% on those sales. You pay your salespeople what you agreed to pay them and there's 50% left over. If that person moves on to something else, that 60% of their business stays with you.

All you need is a really great salesperson out there knocking on doors for you, when you can really as a whole have very passive income where you're really not providing any other services other than your sales person out there.

Joe Grushkin: You're thinking too small. A territory has 30,000 businesses with five to seven salespeople. You've got people working in different parts of a neighborhood and you figure about 4,000-5,000 businesses per salesperson. This is truly a way to own something without having to build it, without having to warehouse it, without needing a huge complex, or staff people, or building websites, or credit card processing, or computer programs. This is a business in a box. It's a 60/40 split where the lion's share going to the marketing arm of the system.

Let's just say I bought a territory and I wanted to have a salesperson out there, do you have marketing information available so they can get started right away? Or, would I have to create that?

Joe Grushkin: Everything is created in a back office. The training is all modularized, so that if you have somebody to train, they would log on and they would know the elevator speech and the getting started mindset in less than an hour. They could be out talking to business owners two hours later, and then come back with 15 or 20 leads. Watch module two (which is 20 minutes long) and know how to enter leads into the system. They'll start getting e-mails which are all pre-written for the Ambassadors. The customer gets the e-mails, opens them, the Ambassador is notified of those e-mails and then there's a script in section three on how to schedule an appointment with those people.

We're getting a 60% appointment acceptance rate from people that we talk to. Six out of ten people accept an appointment, because it's the National Association of Local Businesses calling. Then, we sit down with our client, have a conversation, go through our guided conversation to identify what their needs are, what can we help them with, and to point them to the best products and services available to them to help their needs. And then, this is where the magic is... our Ambassadors don't have to know 100 different products; they just have to know how to point people to the right people who can then do the selling.

Tell me where people can find out more information about that.

Joe Grushkin: To learn more about the National Association of Local Businesses (NAOLB), visit: NAOLB.com. Click on the opportunity tab or the product tab to view all the products we have. Our Ambassador benefits packages with all three entry points are there. All of the contracts are linked to that, so you can see the territory owner contracts. You can see the Ambassador agreement by clicking "Enroll now." There's an opportunity to find out more about the sales process and how we do everything. If somebody wants to get started, they can click a button, and be started literally the next day.

When did you start working with this idea as a business?

Joe Grushkin: The business started in 2011 with the inception of MaxExposure, but it really evolved in 2018. It took almost two years to pull together all the service providers. I refer to it as the Field of Dreams, so if I built it, they would come, and they are the Ambassadors to bring it to their communities.

What an opportunity it is, for even just small businesspeople, or really anybody out there. If readers want to have a secondary passive stream of income it sounds like this may be the perfect opportunity.

Joe Grushkin: Well not only that, but people look at it as, let me kick the tires a little bit, but the real entrepreneurs are the ones who say, "Holy crap, ground floor opportunity?" I mean if you have the opportunity to give Bill Gates $5,000 in 1997 when he was just getting started you might have thought twice about it, but now would you do it? Ground floor things are really very rare and real entrepreneurs see that. They see what the future is, they do their due diligence, and they look at it carefully. But, when you see how low the investment really is, and the upside potential for what can really be done, this is not a part-time "kick the tires" type of thing. This is something that will generate a significant income in 3-4 months. There are very few businesses you can talk about that could be generating a sustainable income in as little as six months!

About Joe Grushkin

Joe Grushkin is the CEO and Founder of the National Association of Local Businesses. His company offers over 100 top quality products and services for local businesses, at discounted pricing normally reserved for much larger companies and membership is free. Joe shares his journey of how he went from a young, ambitious salesperson inducted into the Cutco "Hall of Fame" to becoming the CEO of his own business.

His company, MaxExposure Social Media was founded in 2012 in Westport, CT. MaxExposure Social Media is a Social Media Management company dedicated to helping small and medium sized businesses enhance their social presence online. As a 2nd generation family business, MaxExposure Social Media treats customers as part of the family, often connecting personally through social media to share our lives. MaxExposure offers MORE than just Social Media and Reputation Management. They offer a concierge service that often goes above and beyond the scope of work that has been contracted.

To learn more about Joe Grushkin and the National Association of Local Businesses, go to NAOLB.com.

WEBSITE
NAOLB.com

EMAIL
Joe@NAOLB.com

LINKEDIN
LinkedIn.com/in/JoeGrushkin

FACEBOOK
Facebook.com/JoeGrushkin

PHONE
(203) 247-2008

How to Out-Market and Out-Sell Your Competition: In Good Times and Bad

Jerry Kezhaya grew up in the auto repair business. His father started an automatic transmission repair shop back in Detroit in 1946. Since then, Jerry has been around cars, but he didn't stop there. He went on to create a mastermind, a business mentoring business, a carwash and a strip mall, he is a true serial entrepreneur. He's been recognized and given Small Business Awards and environmental awards as well.

During the Corona virus pandemic, Jerry took the time to share some very specific things with small business owners that may be wondering, will they be able to survive? Will they be able to have a business afterwards? Jerry offered ideas that other business owners will be able to use to help get their business back on track during and after the Corona virus.

Conversation with Jerry Kezhaya

Talk about your auto repair shop first, tell us what's happening and about the calls you're getting asking, "How are you guys still fixing cars and getting business during the Coronavirus pandemic when the economy has been shut down?

Jerry Kezhaya: I wanted to take the time to offer ideas that other business owners will be able to use to help get their business back on track during and after the Corona virus pandemic. COVID-19 has just paused the economy. I'm thinking, "How in the world can you pause the economy and expect people to continue doing business and taking care of their families? That's a question I keep scratching my head about, how do you do that? But that's what they are doing in Washington. I know small business owners can't just pause their business and survive very long and I want to help with my expertise in business marketing.

So, I started this company literally in the driveway of my house in 1981. We have since grown it into the largest independent repair shop in northeast Texas. We are .8 acres under the roof, to give you an example, 35,220 square feet. It's a big shop. I tell everybody, it's a big machine that likes to eat a lot of broken cars and spit them out well repaired and restored on the other end. So, if we take a lot of cars in, we have to stay busy. We've got employees that are depending on us, we have not laid anybody off. We have not reduced anyone's hours. We are just blowing and going. We are not breaking records, but we are certainly keeping our staff busy. We're keeping our all of our folks doing what they need to do.

Our vendors have called us up repeatedly asking, "What in the world are you guys doing? Because you're the only ones that have any cars and everybody else is dead." Other shops have zero cars, and we are taking them in almost as we normally take them in. I'll tell you what it boils down to, in our opinion, and that's just good old-fashioned communication. We are huge proponents of communicating any and every way that you can with your clients.

I'm not joking. We still send out a printed newsletter to our clients. It's something we do every single month. If you're on my list, you're going to be on my list until you tell us to stop. It keeps growing, every month our numbers continue to grow. We send out an email newsletter to our clients every two weeks. We send out reminder postcards. We send out thank you notes. We send hand-written, thank you notes to every single client that comes into the building, regardless of their spend. If we haven't seen our clients in a while, we actually get on the phone and call them. Right now with COVID-19 we are calling our elderly clients, not that we want them to bring their cars in, but what we're doing is calling them up and asking them, "Do you need anything? Do you need help running errands? Do you want us to pick up something for you? We're happy to do that.

We've been part of this community, next January, 40 years. I just think that it's very important for me to give to the community. I think that this is this has been a great town for our businesses. We have been really blessed by having so many companies at one time, my wife and I own seven. Several are multi-million-dollar companies. This year I'll be 62. It's time for me to start winding down and just focusing on a couple businesses. So, I've sold a couple projects that we had and right now we have four companies, so it's really good to be able to really focus my energies back on the things that I truly love.

Like I said, we communicate with our folks. We send them emails, newsletters, we call them, everything that you can think about as far as marketing. The only thing that we're not able to do right now with marketing is handshake networking (due to the pandemic). When you go to Chambers of Commerce and BMI groups, and Rotaries, and that sort of thing, because everything is shut down, but we still continue doing the things that we know will work and how do you know that they'll work? You've got to be really careful.

When you're marketing for new folks, you've got to make sure that number one, you've got the right market, number two, you got to have the right medium. You've got to have the right message. For example, boomers love the printed newsletter, they've got to have something they can hold. Now millennials, if you send it to them in an email, they're all they're all about that. Text messaging is actually even better than an email. Millennials don't care for email as much as texting. Then, you've got to make sure that you're sending the right message.

So again, you've got to know who your market is, you've got to know what medium/media it is that they that they are attracted to and you also have to have the right message. Marketing is a science. You can't just throw money at it and expect it to be effective. People are drowned today in so many marketing pieces that they're starting to turn more of a blind eye to it. So again, the right media, the right market, and the right message are critical.

You have to know who your client is. You have to know exactly who your top clients are, we've created an avatar for our client. We know everything about that type of person who is our client. We just make sure that we're talking to them as if they were sitting here. If they're were on the phone with me right now, what would I be talking to them about when it comes to marketing? That's what we try to focus on and make happen with all of our stuff.

Here's the thing that hurts me so badly with small business owners that you just really dialed way in. First of all, it's all about the list. You have a list. You know who they are, you know their demographics.

Jerry Kezhaya: We have a lot of these small business owners, let's say it's a catering company, that person is cooking and loves food. They don't even have a list. During this period of time, even if they wanted to pick up the phone and call those elderly people, even if they wanted to send a printed newsletter, they don't even know who their customers are. So, I always start there.

The secret is in the list, people. One of the things I've got is a direct mail piece that looks like a man's paper wallet. People will say to me, "Well, what kind of response can I get if I mail that out?" I said, "Well, if you're doing hearing aids, and you're sending to the 80-year-old, you're not going to get any response." So not only do you have to have a list, you've got to know the list.

I want to go back to your printed newsletter. I bet that piece does well because you are right, boomers like printed things coming in the mailbox. I bet that thing is just a fun piece, right? It's not some boring thing, it's crazy. What does this thing look like?

Jerry Kezhaya: Our company colors are yellow and black. Our newsletter comes on yellow paper with black ink. It is a four page. Folded twice so you can mail it easily. It's 11x17. It has almost the exact effect of a full color newsletter, but it's like a third of the cost. And this thing is so beautiful. First of all, I have a service that I work with, it takes me truly about 20 minutes to put this thing together. It goes out every month and there's nothing in it about a car.

It's called "Fuel for Thought," a free monthly newsletter from your friends at the auto shop. In the example I'm looking at we have April events. You have April Fool's Day, Children's Day books, a bunch of little things that are on your calendar, or could be. The next one is "New T-cell may be grown to fight all cancers." Another one is a snapshot of doctor's lifestyles. There's a little square that says, "Do you have a question about car maintenance that you want answered? We'd love to hear from all of our good friends and clients who enjoy reading our monthly newsletter, if you have a question about anything related to your vehicle reach out, and we have our phone number, email, or they can visit our website. At the very bottom of this one, it says, "Save yourself and a friend some money all month long. Give this coupon to a friend." When they bring it in, we'll send you a crisp $25 bill plus give your friend $25 off any service.

So, we're already working on our referral program right on the first page of our newsletter. The second one, we have a thank you. It's for the clients that refer people to us. Then there's more stories on the inside. At the bottom of that page, we have an April showers special, where we're doing special prices on oil changes. The next page, it shows a square and it's "Congratulations to our Client of the Month" and we tell them what they're in there for. Then we've got some cartoons. Another block has a testimonial with a customer's name on it. Page three has more stories— How to Start an Emergency Fund, Dolphins Demonstrate Cooperative Behavior. The third coupon is "Car Care Labor Savings." Three coupons in the whole thing.

On the inside, we have two double sided inserts. The first one says, "Protocol implemented for the Coronavirus." We talk about our night drop off and early, early bird drops. We have a lockbox outside, we put up a cell phone lockbox so that after hours, you can go to our website, pay for your vehicle, and we will put your keys and the invoice inside the lockbox and set the combination to the last four digits of your cell number. This box has eight lockers on it. You don't have to come into the building. We bought hospital sanitizers and before anything happens every morning, we sanitize the entire office, anything that a customer could touch. And then when they come in, we sanitize our pens right in front of them, and they can put it in their pocket and keep it and of course it says our company name, "The Auto Shop" on it and gives our website and phone number. We sanitize their keys, wipe down their vehicle, anything that they could touch.

All of our tech's now are wearing gloves and face masks when they're working on the cars. Once the vehicles done, they get sanitized again and as well as the keys and it's just a seamless process. We use seat covers and steering wheel covers. We're handwashing. If you go to our website, they can go to the bottom of the page and pay via the web on a secure page. We even have six months, same as cash available via our website. So, we're doing lots of things and we're communicating all this our newsletter, right? We remind folks of the care that we're taking to keep not only them safe, but our employees as well. So, it's really pretty cool.

Let me tell you something, this thing purposefully looks hokey. My customers come in here and tell me every month, "Man, I love your newsletter. You do a great job putting that thing together. They think I'm here cutting and pasting and putting it together on my computer."

I'm in a very interesting business. I have a beautiful office. It's nice, but it isn't too nice. If a guy comes in here, and he's driving a Pinto, I can't have my place looking like Taj Mahal because they're going to think I'm overcharging them. So, our place is nice, it isn't over the top, there's no granite, there's nothing fancy. It's the same thing with our newsletter. If I produce a very professional looking full color, beautiful piece that could win awards, it would be over the top. The image of the newsletters sets the tone of the customer's expectation of your price level.

In the auto repair business, I do not ever want anyone to think that I'm the most expensive guy out there. I don't want them to think I'm the cheapest. I just want them to know that we're the best. We have a trivia competition here where they can win a free oil change and we get scores of folks calling us every month trying to win the free oil change. It's one of the things that we continue to do to create continuity with our clients.

For another type of business, maybe it's a different story. If you're working with a different profession, it's different. I've got an attorney client of ours; he does a beautiful full color newsletter. But for what we're doing, we're spending less than $1 per client, per month. I figured out that it cost me about $11.70 a year, including postage per customer, per client to send this out to them. How can I not spend $12 a year on a client to keep them?

It's called "Top of Mind" awareness. I want to make sure that anytime anything happens with their car that they think of me they think of "The Auto Shop." They think of calling us.

Not only have you been extremely successful in your auto business, but you are now a mentor and a mastermind for other businesses. Readers could be somebody who has a dental office, a chiropractic office, somebody who has some other kind of business, or does this kind of marketing work in their business as well. Let's pick the dentist. If you had a dental office, what would you think they should be doing right now?

Jerry Kezhaya: Number one, they've got to be marketing. That's without question. I don't understand why they're not sending out newsletters, if they're not. Dan Kennedy has said it forever, your lowest hanging fruit is your repeat customers. People that already know, love and trust you. Why would you not work on retaining those clients? It cost me almost $100 to capture a new client. $100 every time I want a new client, I have to calculate I'm spending $100. That's a lot of money to get someone come in for a $40 oil change. It cost me $100 they get someone in to do a $40 oil change with the hope that they come back. Well, you know what, it cost me $12 bucks to keep that oil change. They come in twice a year for oil changes plus state inspections plus everything else. Why would I not want to stay in contact with that client?

Right now, with a dental business, I would still do a newsletter. I mean, I haven't heard from my dentist. They sent me a thing in six months that it's time to come back in for a cleaning. But I haven't heard from them. They haven't called. They haven't sent me a newsletter. Their marketing is terrible in my opinion. They're so busy trying to get new people, they don't care about the old people, their current clients, they hope that they just come back magically. You have to, everybody is reaching out. Dental offices here have just exploded in the numbers in our area. I'm getting all kinds of marketing postcards, and coupons to come in. I'm not a coupon shopper or anything, but I'm looking because I'm in marketing. I want to see what people are sending out, right? So, I check my mailbox every single day and I look at every single piece. If there's something that's beautiful that I really like, I'm going to call them up in a couple weeks and say, how did that piece do for you? I'm in a different business, or I'll even go visit the office manager because I'm a student of marketing, I want to know the best thing out there that is really working.

If you don't have your avatar dialed in, if you don't know exactly who your clients are, if you don't know exactly who your top 10% of your clients are, you're gonna piss away so much money and have such poor results. And you will think, this marketing stuff sucks. It doesn't work. It's just a waste of money. I'm spending $12 a year on clients and my retention rates are pretty high. I'm pretty amazed with it. We know who we market to. I know exactly who my avatar is. I know exactly where my top 10 clients live. When you have it lasered in, it makes all the difference in the world, instead of spending $100 per client, I spent $12.

Right now, during the Corona virus pandemic, most of us are huddled in our houses and we are not even driving. So why would I bring my car to your location at this particular time, just because it's time for my oil change? Why are they coming to you?

Jerry Kezhaya: Well, what they're telling us is, this is the perfect time to bring their vehicle in to us. Number one, we send them the reminders, and we call them up. We're doing our marketing as normal. They look around and say, "You know what, it's a great time to bring my car into the shop. I won't be needing it. I don't have to worry about a ride to work. I don't have to worry about renting a car. I don't have to worry about trying to pick up my kids from school, this is the perfect time to get my car work done." We have a shuttle service, we pick them up, we take them, we pick up their car, we drop their car off, we can pick when the customer comes in, if they prefer for us to give them a ride, we will give them a ride in one of our vehicles.

There are so many opportunities to market right now. There are so many people, you have a captive audience. They're home. They're glued to their computers. They're watching the news. They're poring over Twitter and Facebook and Instagram and every other social media platform out there. What better time to market when you have people's eyes, craving something other than Corona news? Back in the early to mid-70s. My dad was had his shop going, he had converted to a full general repair shop we and we did transmissions and I was reading one of our trade magazines and it was the greatest. It was life changing for me. I cannot stress this enough. It was life changing. The trade magazine on the cover had a picture of a guy halfway under a car from his waist down. You can the top part of his shirt and the boots and everything. He was laying on a creeper halfway underneath the car and he had the coiled phone cord with him. The headline said, "You Cannot Run Your Business from a Creeper." I looked at that and I said, "Dad, this is real. I've got to follow this; this is my destiny. I'm going to run the business." My dad looked at me, he said, "All those people are crazy. They don't know what they're talking about." Well, let me tell you something. It was life changing for me. I was a great tech. Notice I said *was*, I wouldn't hold a candle to the techs I've got today. If I had to go out there and work on a car, I'd be in trouble because of all the changes. But, I'm an amazing business owner running seven companies simultaneously, while averaging 126 days a year traveling. And having each company continue to grow while we're doing it. This is running a business. It's not working in the business. You can't run a business, if you're doing the work. You can't run a restaurant, if you're the cook. You can't run a pest control company, if you're the guy doing the applications. You can't run a law firm, if you're the guy making all the contracts. You can't do it. You have to pick your master; you have to pick the one thing that you can be the best at and run with it to become the best you can be. And like the story says, you can't have your cake and eat it too. You cannot be the best technician and the best business owner. It's impossible.

You do a lot of business when you have the seven businesses. Do you do a lot with systems? Is that how you were able to travel for 126 days and still run the business?

Jerry Kezhaya: Everything is systematized. We have we have our processes and procedures for every one of the companies online. Every one of the procedures is on our network servers. It's also in a binder, and each department head, or area has their own. We call them Standard Operating Procedures (SOP's), and every group has its own SOP's. It's how we do everything. It's as detailed as, "You entered the building at the north facing door, turn the key counter-clockwise until it clicks and you can remove the key, remove the key, open the door," this is all part of the process. "As you open the door, turn the lights on at the switch on your left and go to the alarm panel. Enter your code." This is how detailed our processes are. And every one of them is a living document. We update it. We just went through our accounting package and updated it completely, two weeks ago. Everything is systematized everything has a process to it and every process is documented.

If you don't do that, you're just setting yourself up to be a person dependent company, as opposed to a systems dependent company. I have a one of our clients, he ran a bakery. He fell into a diabetic coma and he was in ICU for 11 weeks. It was six months before he could walk again and go back into his building. He had to learn to talk again. He had to learn to walk, and he had to learn how to write. He was like a baby when he came out of the coma. I said, "How did you stay in business?" He said, "I just did what you told me." I said, "What are you talking about?" He says, "Look, here's my binder." It had every recipe it. It had every oven setting, how you clean the ovens, how you how you do everything for the bakery, and he had his kids and some part time help running the business for him. He said, "Look, I wasn't breaking records, but they kept the lights on for me while I got better." That, my friends, is the most important thing that I can tell you about having systems and Standard Operating Procedures. It will keep your business going when you can't be there.

My wife and I had the most amazing gal working for us. Her name was Linda and Linda was my friend. She worked with us for nine years. Linda was my right arm; she ran the businesses when I wasn't here. She took care of all the books, the payroll, she handled the entire back end of the business. She ran the offices, took care of everybody. She was the go between, between me and every other employee. They didn't ask me for stuff, they asked Linda. Well, one Sunday night I got a phone call. Linda died at 7:30 that Sunday night, and I had never even opened our QuickBooks program. My wife and I got to the office the next morning at 6 am. By 6:20, we had payroll done for all of the companies because we had it in the system. It was in the Standard Operating Procedures. I would not be in business today, if I did not have those SOP's.

This has to come from the top, down. For anybody that works for you, it is not a suggestion. It's not when you get around to it, it is absolutely required, without question. We have to do this. Not only do we have to do it, but it's ongoing. If there's ever something that needs to be updated, we fix it immediately. If you find, "Oh, hey, we got a new credit card processing machine, We have to change our systems now. We have to change our SOP's to reflect the new buttons that have to be pushed for the for the reports that you need at the end of the day." When anything like that happens, it's updated because, what happens if you have someone who is your vender, and your vender passes away? Who's going to help you? You've got to be able to run the business regardless of whether that employee shows up or doesn't show up.

You're the marketer who's saying anything that comes in my mailbox, I'm looking at it. Have you seen anything really creative right now during this time that caught your eye?

Jerry Kezhaya: I have not seen anything that has been creative, coming across my desk. Nothing. What I'm looking at is as if it is going to be business as usual. And this is not business as usual. You're going to have to do something to jump outside of the normal.

In our local newspaper, usually there's lots of inserts stuffed in it. There was there was only one piece that was stuffed in our local newspaper on Sunday, we have 300,000 population, we're fairly large suburb. I'm seeing people stopping their marketing, stopping. We're putting the foot on the gas; I'm adding more to it. My wife says, "What are you doing now? Are you kidding?"

Crank up that voiceless or the ringless voicemail. I want to make that work for us right now. We're starting things we've never tried. I'm working on something that I really like, lumpy mail. I like lumpy mail for lots of reasons and we're I'm putting together a pretty fun piece we're going to get these little socks. You can buy a pair of socks for $.50 online and they're little kid socks. I'm putting together a piece that's going to say, "For service that'll knock your socks off." We'll put that in there and people will feel the lumpy mail and be like, "What is that?" and open it to see. That's just one of the things that we're thinking about.

I'm the queen of lumpy mail. You're talking my language now. Do you belong to a mastermind? Are you hearing anything from your mastermind members who are also very brilliant marketers, any cool stories? Any cool ideas?

Jerry Kezhaya: Right now, I belong to three mastermind groups. I lead one currently and looking to grow into leading two. I'm basically a business marketing specialist. That's really what I do. We've got we got our businesses basically running on autopilot. We've got good people, and good systems. I get to do the marketing and I'm always reaching out. I have not honestly seen or heard anything lately that makes me say, "Wow, I'm gonna swipe and deploy that today." I see my email is blowing up, and all everybody wants to talk about is COVID-19. We hear enough about that. I'm burned out on that, show me something different man.

I understand. The funny thing is, I worked at Notre Dame for a number of years. I was in the purchasing department, and one of the things I was responsible for was buying copiers. We had a fleet of 400 copiers. Can you believe that, even though I've now done multi-million-dollar marketing for Notre Dame, one time, I was in charge of buying copiers. I said, "Who is your number one salesperson?" And, he said, "Well, it's this woman down in Florida." I said, "What does she do different than everybody else?" That was always my question. What do they do different than everybody else. he says, "She produces this crazy ugly newsletter! All she did was talk about her vacation or random things; it was nothing that connected to selling anything.

You talked about wanting to have a second mastermind. If somebody was interested in your mastermind, do you have a way that they could connect?

Jerry Kezhaya: Go to BBmmusa.com. That stands for Business Builder, Mentor and Mastermind USA. I have clients from New Hampshire to Washington State and lots of places in the middle. It's an amazing group of really smart businesspeople dedicated to helping each other achieve success and focused on helping businesses survive during and after the Coronavirus pandemic and thrive into the future.

About Jerry Kezhaya

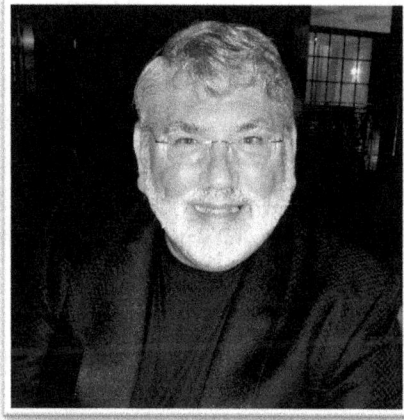

Jerry Kezhaya is the serial entrepreneur behind The Auto Shop, Business Builders Mentor & Mastermind, My Car Wash, Jupiter Parkway Village, Ltd, and Texas Wine Posse. Jerry was born in Detroit, Michigan. His father opened the first automatic transmission repair shop in Detroit, in 1946. This is where Jerry first learned how to work on cars. Jerry started his first company in New York in 1979 which he sold to his business partner.

Jerry then moved to Plano, TX in August 1980 with the purpose of starting The Auto Shop. The Auto Shop began in January 1981 and is currently the largest independent auto repair facility in northeast Texas. Jerry was presented the award for Small Businessperson of the Year in May 1999 and was the Texas State winner of the US Chamber of Commerce Blue Chip Enterprise Award in September 2000. The Auto Shop was awarded the Environmental Star of Excellence from the city of Plano in 2005 and Jerry was awarded Texas Environmentalist of the Year in 2006.

Jerry is very involved in the community. He was the charter president for the Central Plano Chapter of AMBUCS and the Chairman for the Tuxedos and Trykes Black Tie Gala. He has been involved with The City of Plano and its Boards and Commissions for almost 15 years. He has been the Chairman of the Board of Adjustment and a Planning and Zoning Commissioner for the City of Plano, Chairman of the Collin County Parks Foundation Board, Chairman of the North Texas Chamber of Commerce, and served on the Transition and Revitalization Commission. Jerry was a member of Board of Directors, the Executive Board, the Finance Committee, and Chair of Government Relations Committee for the Plano Chamber of Commerce, as well as the Chair for the Citizen of the Year Celebration and the Chair for the Women's Division Homecoming Fund Raising Gala. Jerry is an advisory member for the Plano Symphony, an active volunteer for Muscular Dystrophy and numerous other groups.

Jerry is married to Dr. Laura Shwaluk and he is also the father of two.

WEBSITE
TheAutoShop.com

EMAIL
jerrykezhaya@yahoo.com

FACEBOOK:
Facebook.com/Jerry.Kezhaya

Embracing Change to Survive and Thrive in a Changing Business World

Mike Stewart is president and founder of Stewart Internet Solutions Inc., an internet consulting agency and services company located in Nashville, TN. Mike has composed countless radio jingles, television scores, and produced or performed music heard all over the world. He has worked with world famous musicians such as Tommy Roe, Joe South, William Bell (Georgia Hall of Fame Recipient and 2017 Grammy Winner), Buckner Garcia, Atlanta Rhythm Section, Billy Joe Royal, Alicia Bridges, Isaac Hayes, Eddie Floyd, Bertie Higgins, Doug Johnson, and Bill Anderson. He has a gold record for playing keys on 1980's hit, "Pac-Man Fever" as a band member of Buckner & Garcia and recorded the theme to Disney's Oscar nominated movie, "Wreck-It Ralph" in 2012.

He owned and operated a recording studio for over twenty years working in all facets of digital audio and video. In 1996, Mike became passionate about the future of the Internet and how small businesses could benefit from the web if they just understood how to make it work for their company. He saw how the broadcast of audio and video information on a website was no different than the television/radio industry he had been a part of all his life. Since that time, he has become very successful consulting with small business owners on how to set up their worldwide TV stations and broadcast their unique marketing message to the world.

Conversation with Mike Stewart

Mike, tell us about yourself and your business. Let's talk about how business owners can embrace change to help their businesses survive and thrive during the Coronavirus pandemic.

Mike Stewart: I hope that when people read this that the Coronavirus pandemic has passed and we're on a recovery path where the economy's restored and people are back to living life. But, I think that this is a wakeup call for small businesses to change the way to find customers and make money. There are strategies that small business owners for one reason or another, just didn't want to embrace until now. Now is the time when it is most important to embrace change to keep your business alive.

I have two types of local business clients that I've worked with, those that are willing to do what it takes to get to get what needs to be done and those that don't believe it's worth doing and procrastinate and look at it as overwhelming and say, "I'll never do that."

They have an inclination; I want to hire somebody to do that for me. Or, they think it's not worth doing. A lot of people even when they were told "this is the path," for one reason or another didn't embrace it. One of the things that's been interesting to me is, the world is now realizing that there are different ways, and in some ways, better ways of doing things.

I've known about Zoom since the beginning. I use GoToWebinar, WebEx, Zoom, Skype, StreamYard. If there's a virtual meeting tool, I know about it or used it. They're just tools. In the networking days of building relationships with brick and mortar local businesses, you'd say, "Hey, would you like to meet virtually?" And more times than not people would say, "No, I like to be face-to-face with people so you need to come to my place of business and let's set up a meeting." Now, all the sudden, I'm getting in the car driving across town because I want to build a relationship of "know, like and trust" with a local business owner. I kept thinking, I could really be more efficient if I was using something like Zoom, or GoToMeeting. Now this pandemic has made the whole world discover Zoom. It went to over 200 million users overnight. When you bring in new technologies, new strategies, new ideas, change is hard for people. It's not a criticism. It's not complaining, it's just an observation. I've just always been somebody that embraced change.

When you get into my music history, I owned a recording studio starting in 1979. That's over 41 years ago, I started my recording studio. Back then, to record audio was a technological strategy. There was a learning curve. Everybody in the room didn't know how to professionally record and I became an audio engineer. There were no schools for it. You had to either be an apprentice working at a studio, or learn through the school of hard knocks (which I did a little bit of all of that.) And so I have 41 years history of understanding how audio, video, advertising and marketing work on those technologies called radio and television. And then along comes the Internet. And I said, "Oh my gosh, the Internet's nothing more than television for everybody. It's radio and television!" Now, traditional television and radio are diminishing because the world listens to streaming audio and streaming video, which are the new tech—

they're just delivery methods. The content creation side still takes people to be creative and create content that people want to connect with. When you bring all these technologies and the delivery methods into the equation with local business owners, I've got a top 10 strategy I teach. Local businesses don't pay attention to the changes in technology and delivery systems. So, I love to share those things.

Let's share with the readers a couple of those strategies. I know you've mentioned before that you have two types of business owners that work with you, one that said, "Yep, I'm going to do everything you say, and I'm going to get it done." And then there were others that said, "Well, Mike, I don't have the time. I'm just not very good at it. I don't have the money…"

It's probably my guess the people right now that are in the worst situation are those in the second category, am I right?

Mike Stewart: Absolutely, and it breaks my heart. The people that are in small businesses that cannot practice their trade right now—plumbers, service industries, people that are in service-based businesses. My heart goes out to those that have been deemed "non-essential." Sadly, the music industry is "non-essential." Therefore, there's no live performances, there's no restaurants open. There's no travel allowed. This is the first month in 40 years I've gotten by on one tank of gas.

No amount of marketing is going to fix those things. But when the economy recovers, there are lots of businesses that will reopen —the total economy is not going to be destroyed. But, what happens is, there's a lot of businesses that should have embraced some of these strategies. My business clients that are local businesses, which are majority of them, are in service businesses, particularly pest control. They're slammed with business because of the strategies. They're being found. They're getting called. And, they are necessary.

All of our pest control clients that did the things we told them to do. The phone is ringing off the wall, because people are home to finding problems. Nobody wants to live with rodents and pests. They are assuring people that they can safely treat their homes from the outside and keep them safe. So, strategy number one that I tell every local business, "Understand Google Business Services." It's free. It's used to be called Google Maps, Google Places. First, I ask, "Are you listed?" It's important because it's where people praise you or complain about you. I look at customers every day that never pay attention to it. They have nothing but horrible reviews, one-star reviews. A lot of people said I'd give you zero stars if I could. The bottom is one star and the top is five stars. We tell all of our clients, "Don't ignore your Google business listing. Claim your listing, you should have been all along asking for five-star reviews. All of our clients have 100 plus five-star reviews. Therefore, when people are looking for these essential services, they're ranking very high, the very first thing you see. The pecking order with Google is paid ads, the six pack and then organic search. Many people say, "I never looked at that. I've got a person who handles it." Well, I can look at and tell you in 30 seconds if it's been handled. It's amazing how many businesses have ignored this and it's hurting them.

So how do they get to the people to actually do the reviews? How do they make it easy for them to do that?

Mike Stewart: Number one, when they are one of our clients, we make a clickable link that works on cell phones, tablets and computers, that says, "Review me on Google." It's one tap. They can give you a negative or a positive review, one star or five stars. But Google will not allow anybody that doesn't have a Google login or Gmail address, to give a review. You have to be diligent with your good customers and do whatever you can. If you can come up with an incentive to get them to give a review, do that. We're told not to say that, but let's put it this way, do whatever you can to get five-star reviews. Make it easy, have a link on your website that people can tap on their phone. Even something as simple as, "Nina does an amazing job, I recommend her." That's a great review.

So Mike, you're saying if somebody has an AOL account, AOL email or Yahoo, they can't leave a review?

Mike Stewart: They have to have a Gmail account or Google account. They have to be logged into their Google account to leave a review. What you do if some people don't have a Google account and can't review a review is, you keep asking. You get 100 reviews and when you get to 100, you keep going. There's millions of people in your market with Gmail addresses. I have a client who has done 1600 five-star reviews in the city of Tampa. Don't tell me, there's not 1600 people in the city Nashville, that could give you a positive review. I'm just asking for 100. That's realistic. I don't care if it takes you three months to do it, six months to do it. It is a strategy that is life or death for your business.

You don't stop at 100, you keep going. Let's say you got to 100, two years ago and then you've never asked again. That also wouldn't be good, would it?

Mike Stewart: Absolutely not. Do you need to breathe to live? Why would you stop at 100 and say, "Well, I'm done breathing." This is the lifeblood of your Internet presence. 96% of the world finds local businesses on their cell phones and they make a decision to call you or not, sometimes from just your Google reviews or Yelp reviews. You really need to do it on Facebook, Yelp and Google. You need to do all three. You need high praise at all the review sites. And that's all part of reputation management.

I teach the world my "SERP" term. SERP is a search engine optimization (SEO) term meaning Search Engine Results Page (SERP). It means people type words into Google or Bing or Yahoo or whatever search engine and those are the words that people use, they are generic search terms. Here's an example, a roofer near me, a real estate agent near me, those are generic search terms. However, to get on the first page of the search engines for those generic terms is really competitive, and pretty unlikely. However, a lot of businesses have search terms that guarantee that they will dominate, for that search result, they will be the dominant results.

If you could go to Google right now and type in websites, I dominate the page of Google for "websites you control." We discovered that lots of local businesses control a few words. For example, one of my clients is Canton termite. He dominates Google all over the world for those search terms. So that is a strategy that has helped a client like Canton termite dominate during these times. He has 100 plus reviews. He's told me many times and he always asked, "Why did you call me?" They said, "Well, your reviews were through the roof." He said, "I can't calculate the amount of money I've made by that. He markets all over his local market his search terms, if you need pest control, Google "Canton termite." That's it. Search "Canton termite" and you will find him.

Search terms are a valuable strategy that you can market through a multitude of media. We actually do it with music. I created something called SERP music, which is a jingle, a piece of music with your search terms set to music, so that when people hear your radio and TV and YouTube and Spotify audio ads, and even audio ads on Facebook, they're hearing in their subconscious, your search terms. In fact, the lyrics are "Google Canton, Termite and Pest Control, no bug will survive." And then you put their phone number and we sing their phone number, and it makes it dead easy on a subconscious level using power of music to teach your local market their search terms. That's one of the reasons I'm an advocate of using music to market search terms.

What you're saying is even, let's say it's a chiropractor, and the chiropractor listened to you and got 5-star reviews and used Google Business and search terms will survive and thrive in these times. Versus chiropractor who said, "Well, I rarely check my reviews online. I just treat the patients," who will be struggling right now.

Mike Stewart: In fact, I've got a chiropractor in Gainesville, Georgia. We did a jingle. He's Dr. Jack Winner. His jingle was, "Winner Wellness Center" and his jingle says "Google Winner wellness" just like a winner of a ballgame. He dominates the first page of Google for Winner Wellness. Nobody else in the world dominates like he does. He markets his search term through YouTube advertising, paid advertising. He does Google AdWords.

Another strategy I want to share—we knew years ago in Internet marketing that blogging was an organic content marketing strategy. Meaning, the more content you create and put on your website, the higher you can rank for all kinds of search terms in Google. It was a strategy called "Blog and Pain." It required you being a good writer, in other words, people were reading your content. I'll be honest with you, I've never been a good writer. I don't like writing. I used to hate term papers. But, I love sharing knowledge.

Seth Godin recently said podcasting is the new blogging. It's easier to speak and transcribe than it is to write. So, Dr. Winter has the "Winter Wellness" podcast on Apple and Spotify, on Android, on Google podcasts on Stitcher, on Alexa. In other words, he's telling his local market to get tips for staying healthy from he and his wife, who is a certified nutritionist. Their podcast is advertising their business and its content marketing, which is raising their Internet presence on a local level, because they're willing to produce a weekly podcast and blog. That's another strategy most businesses can use.

One of the most common objections I get is, "I don't have time." Well, you've got time now. "I don't have a budget." Well, either budget time or money or it never happens. "I don't want to do it." Well, okay, I don't want to eat healthy. I was told to eat healthy and I would be feel better if I did. It's just the part of the way of making things happen. And then "I just overwhelmed." And "I want you to do it for me." I can't be you. I'm not an expert in health. I'm not an expert at pest control. I'm not an expert at plumbing, or roofing. I'm not a chef. I'm not a restaurant. In other words, I'm not you.

I know Internet audio. That's my specialty. I can talk about that all day long. But you have to create original content, proving you're the authority. When you prove you're the authority, you can say "Oh, by the way, here's how you can get in touch with me and do business with me and we want to do business with people that we know, that authority. We like them, we trust them and we feel like we know them.

What happens is, I have a formula with podcasting, blogging, give 80% of amazing content away, proving you're the authority and 20% of the time, tell people in a commercial how to find you, like you, trust you, subscribe to you and buy from you. That formula works for everyone. I would go to customers and say, "You need to do a podcast now. You just sound like you're trying to sell me something." If you said, "I want to be found more." Well, you need to do content marketing. A lot. If you say, "I don't want to do it. I've got a social media person that does that for me." Okay, great. Are they really creating unique, original content?

Sadly, too many people are just posting stuff on social media, like "Happy Birthday" and, "Don't forget, it's Mother's Day." That's not original helpful content, that's just repurposing the obvious. Content marketing is about answering questions with authority and positioning yourself as somebody who knows what you're talking about, and remind them, you're the person to trust, to do business with. That's what local businesses do podcasts for. All of our pest control agencies are seeing a rise in the search engines and their phones are ringing because people are liking the podcast about pest control. The pest control marketing podcast is the number one lead generator for all the new business we get.

Another strategy is to "Become an Authority Site." The only way you can become an authority site is by posting fresh content. Most people get a local business website and never ask themselves, "Is this homepage converting strangers into customers?" Most times, most websites I see for local businesses are just gorgeous, colorful brochures that sell nothing. Once again, we focus on blogging, podcasting, text message marketing. We use a company called Twilio that makes it dirt cheap to give away free content, coupons, incentives to do business, straight to their cell phones merely by dialing a phone number. There's a new website called Repurpose (repurpose.io) that I'm really excited about. I'm using it personally. It lets me take my podcast and repurpose it. I can post to all the social media sites with the click of a mouse if you build templates and then you upload the RSS feed from your podcast to this system.

I've heard if you don't post organically on Facebook, LinkedIn, Twitter and Instagram, if you try to use some sort of a service, it reduces the engagement. Do you agree or disagree?

Mike Stewart: Not when it's audio content, like a podcast, or some other content that is unique. I want to take my podcast and repurpose it on YouTube, Instagram, LinkedIn, Facebook, and to business pages and to business groups. Not so much on my personal social media where, your wife and the grandkids check in, and everybody looks at what they had for dinner last night. I saw today everybody's posting their senior pictures and then a report came out that it's dangerous because scammers are using that to steal identity. So remember, there's business social media, and there's personal social media and don't mix them together.

When I'm repurposing my podcast, as opposed on my business page or in my private group, we have engagement because we built trust. Because of this tool, I can make a podcast and easily put it up on my YouTube channel.

Another strategy I want to share here is "Optimizing Paid Advertising." There are so many places to buy eyes and ears, Google AdWords, Bing ads, Yahoo ads, but probably one of the most overlooked opportunities is YouTube pre-roll advertising. What we're doing with a lot of our local clients is we're buying local TV ads on YouTube, with SERP term jingles. What's great about this is we preload the ads with the search term jingle. In other words, it opens with a search term jingle, has a direct response ad in the middle, and then closes with the search term jingle. 90% of the people skip the ad on YouTube. If you've seen this on YouTube, you're looking for a video about x, y, z and most people skip the ad. Well guess what? You still hear the search terms. "Google Canton Termite and Pest Control." We don't care if they skip the ad. Because they're hearing in their local mall, I can go into YouTube and say only run this ad within a 40-mile radius of my zip code. It's dirt cheap advertising using search term jingles on cell phones. We use this when people are searching YouTube, and then Spotify. Pandora has paid advertising. Of course we put our jingle ads in our own podcast. We say, "Now here's a word from our sponsor," and we run our jingle and we run our ad and then we come back to our show. It's my podcast, so the only advertiser on my podcast is me.

Another strategy that's exciting for local businesses is the resurgence of QR codes. QR codes are those funny little squares with lots of checkers in them. The reason they failed when they came out

10 years ago, is people had to download a special QR code app to make them work. And people didn't understand it. It was clumsy to use. Within the last year, all of the manufacturers, Android and iPhone both have made the camera and the actual phone itself know how to use a QR code. So now all you do is act like you're going to take a picture of it and the QR code responds on your phone. It's never been easier to push content to a phone with QR codes. You can put QR codes on shirts, giveaways, coffee cups, brochures, I actually do them in webinars. I tell people pull out your phone, point it at the slide and I can send you anywhere on the Internet. I can push a phone number to you, I can push anything imaginable. This is one of the things that our customers do that have made a huge connectivity difference, by driving their local market to secret offers, coupons, you name it.

It's an underutilized opportunity because you have to remember, 96% of the world finds local businesses on cell phones, not computers. In fact, when we look at the stats of our advertising, over 90% of the response is coming from phones. I tell people every day, "A phone is a computer, 1 million times more powerful than the computer that the rocket that landed the man on the moon happened to have on it." You've got to start thinking of it as an Internet connected computer that you market to.

These are the kinds of strategies that most local businesses either didn't have time for, didn't pay attention to, or weren't ready to embrace, until now. Now is the time to really start paying attention to it because the people who are willing to do what it takes to make it happen can really come out ahead when this has all passed.

If someone wanted to hire you to do one of those SERP jingles, do you do work outside of your local Nashville area?

Mike Stewart: Oh, absolutely. In fact, we sold a jingle yesterday in Australia to a pest control agency. That's been a blessing to me and my wife, since we have virtual businesses and we can do business anywhere in the world. That's one of the things I think has spurred so many local businesses to change, restaurants, when they couldn't serve food, they went from making a living one night to zero income overnight. Their wish is to hurry up and get back in business. But for us, we can do business everywhere and of course, the businesses that had email lists and text message lists, they could communicate with their local market and creating new things. Maybe they offered cooking classes, or had gift cards for sale, they could have informed their local customers how to do curbside pickup. Many were on Uber Eats, Grubhub and there was an opportunity to expand or get into these systems. I try to help my customers become is virtually connected and create as many things that you can offer all over the world versus just in your backyard. The list goes on and on the things that people could and should do.

We're all trying to sell something. That's how the economy works. When you have nothing to sell, your economy stops. That's what I'm passionate about, trying to help everybody have multiple streams of income. Don't ignore the power of connectivity with the Internet. And, you don't have connectivity with the Internet if you have no Internet presence.

Have they embraced having some sort of a membership or changing what they offer to be more virtually based? Have they moved into that area as well?

Mike Stewart: Well, as Dan Kennedy used to say, "Some will, some won't." The ones that work with us have. Every business is different. Some can work, they were still considered essential services. Other businesses rank very poorly on Google, even though they're an essential business. They're not found, they don't have an email list. They're not connecting with the local market. I actually had one stop his advertising. You know, this is the worst time to stop advertising. This is the time to do everything, anything you can to stand out from the crowd. That's why we contacted all of our existing customers, and we put what was called a red top bar "COVID-19." A disclaimer to let customers know that they're aware of this and they're going to keep their customers safe when they have a problem. There's so many things that you can use the Internet to stay in touch and build that great relationship with customers on a local or a worldwide level.

All you can do is, do the best you can to get to get as much business coming in the door. And, start embracing things that you know. I heard years ago, "Do what you fear." People get overwhelmed with this stuff because it just seems like it's too hard, it's too scary. "I don't like technology. I'm technically challenged." We're all technically challenged if we don't know how to do it. It's, "Are you willing to do what it takes time and budget wise to get past what you don't know?" When somebody says, "I'm technically challenged," my answer is, "Yeah, when it comes to flying an airplane, I'm technically challenged. I just don't choose to invest the time and money to learn to fly a plane, I'll hire a pilot. But if I wanted to learn to fly a plane, I could do it if I really wanted to."

If somebody wanted to get ahold of you, how can they connect?

Mike Stewart: Well, the easiest way in the world is go to websitesyoucontrolyourself.com. In fact, my red bar at the top of my website has over $400 worth of free gifts. You don't even have to opt-in or anything, you don't have to tell me who you are. If you go to the website websitesyoucontrolyourself.com, everything I do is linked right from that website. I'm actually looking for folks that want to be a rep in your local, because I think there's millions of search angles that don't exist and they need to in the coming months and years.

I'm kind of the guy that has brought Music City USA to the Internet world and that's why I moved to Nashville because there's so much amazing talent here. In 2012, my band partner Jerry called me one day and he said, "You're never going to believe the call I got today!" He said, "Disney called!" Well, that's a good call. He said, "I've got some movie called "Wreck-It Ralph" and they it's about 1980s video games." And they said, "Would we be available to record the theme song as if it was "Pac-Man Fever?" I said, "Well, sure. Let's do it, Jerry." He said, "Well, unfortunately, our lead singer had passed away a few years prior. He said, "Well, as long as you're Buckner & Garcia, that's what we want in the movie. We knew you had a hit record, "Pac-Man Fever" in 1980. We think you'd be great to do a theme song for "Wreck-It Ralph."

That was September of 2012. "We'll do it," I said. "We'll get our old drummer, we'll get everybody that's still around together and we'll record the song." They said, "Oh, by the way, we need it in two weeks." So, we recorded it on our computers and uploaded it to Los Angeles. By Thanksgiving when the movie came out, we were in the movie. That's how we got to do it. Because of the Internet!

We were able to record it at home, send it to Los Angeles over the Internet, and it got in the movie. It was the last piece of music in the movie. It's funny, we went to the theater to hear our theme song and by the time it got to the credits where our song played, the theater was empty, so I guess nobody's ever heard it!

About Mike Stewart

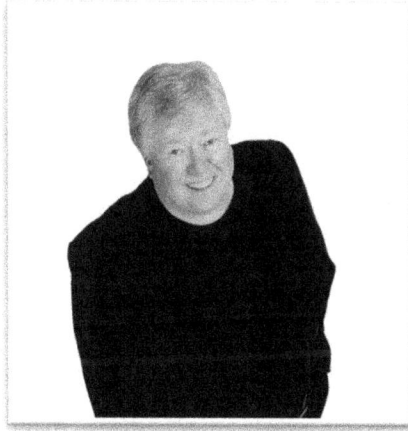

Mike Stewart is president and founder of Stewart Internet Solutions Inc., an internet consulting agency and services company located in Nashville, TN. Mike has composed countless radio jingles, television scores, and produced or performed on music heard all over the world. He has worked with world famous musicians such as Tommy Roe, Joe South, William Bell (Georgia Hall of Fame Recipient and 2017 Grammy Winner), Buckner Garcia, Atlanta Rhythm Section, Billy Joe Royal, Alicia Bridges, Isaac Hayes, Eddie Floyd, Bertie Higgins, Doug Johnson, and Bill Anderson. He has a gold record for playing keys on the 1980's hit, "Pac-Man Fever" as a band member of Buckner & Garcia and recorded the theme to Disney's Oscar nominated movie, "Wreck-It Ralph" in 2012.

The list goes on and on of national performers in the Who's Who. He owned and operated a recording studio for over twenty years working in all facets of digital audio and video. In 1996, Mike became passionate about the future of the Internet and how small businesses could benefit from the web if they just understood how to make it work for their company. He saw how the broadcast of audio and video information on a website was no different than the television/radio industry he had been a part of all his life.

Since that time, he has become very successful consulting with small business owners on how to set up their worldwide TV stations and broadcast their unique marketing message to the world. Stewart Internet Solutions focused on Internet technologies that allowed audio and video to be streamed over the Internet. Internet Solutions developed distance training websites, e-commerce projects, and audio/video intensive web projects utilizing HTML 5 responsive web programming. They didn't stop there, but constantly strive to be on the cutting edge of technology, always searching for better, more efficient ways of achieving their goals.

After listening to a set of audiotapes in 2000, Mike attended his first Internet Marketing seminar. Initially, Mike was a student himself. Soon he was hired to record seminars, events and webinars. Through techniques he learned from the seminar speakers and promoters he was able to create his own software products that made the process easier. While he had spoken to many groups, associations, and business organizations throughout the years, his first Internet Marketing Seminar speaking engagement was in 2003. Since then he has attended and spoken at many events worldwide.

Mike teaches attendees the benefits of owning the right equipment and utilizing it to record themselves to make quality multimedia audio and video information products that can be marketed for high profits. He is always on the lookout for new innovative ideas, products, hardware and software to benefit his clients. His hands-on customer service approach outshines most, and he creates in-depth audio and video tutorials to enhance the products he sells.

Mike and his wife, Susan who works and travels with him on his speaking engagements, now enjoy working with the music industry professionals in Nashville and he has gone back to his passion of song writing and music production. They have three children involved in several aspects of the business.

WEBSITE
WebsitesYouControlYourself.com

EMAIL
mike@internetaudioguy.com

LOCATION
Nashville, TN